# The Successful Writer's Handbook

**By**
**Patricia L. Fry**

**Matilija Press**
**PMB 123**
**323 E. Matilija St., Ste. 110**
**Ojai, CA 93023**
www.matilijapress.com
MatilijaPr@aol.com

# The Successful Writer's Handbook

Second Edition Revised
Copyright © 2003 by Patricia Fry

First Edition published as an ebook in 2002

**Publisher's Cataloging-in-Publication**
 *(Provided by Quality Books, Inc.)*


Fry, Patricia L., 1940
   The successful writer's handbook / by Patricia L.
Fry. — 2nd ed. rev.
   p.cm.
   Includes index.
   ISBN 09612642-7-6

   1. Authorship—Handbooks, manuals, etc. I. Title.

PN153.F792003        808'.02
                     QBIO3-200582

Cover and interior design by Dennis Mullican

# Other Books by Patricia

**A Writer's Guide to Magazine Articles for Book Promotion and Profit** (Matilija Press, 2000)

**Over 75 Good Ideas for Promoting Your Book** (Matilija Press, 2000)

**A Young Writer's Handbook** (Matilija Press, 2003)

**Quest For Truth: A Journey of the Soul** (Matilija Press, 1995)

**The Ojai Valley, An Illustrated History** (Matilija Press, 1983; revised, 1999)

**Nordhoff Cemetery: Book One** (Matilija Press, 1992)

**Nordhoff Cemetery: Book Two** (Matilija Press, 2003)

**A Thread to Hold: The Story of Ojai Valley School** (Fithian Press, 1995)

**The Mainland Luau: How to Capture the Flavor of Hawaii in Your Own Backyard** (Matilija Press, 1995)

**Entertainment Hawaiian Style** (Island Heritage, 1999)

**Creative Grandparenting Across the Miles: Ideas for Sharing Love, Faith and Family Traditions** (Liguori Publications, 1997)

**Write On! Journal-Keeping for Teens** (Liguori Publications, 2001)

**Youth Mentoring: Sharing Your Gifts With the Future** (Liguori Publications, scheduled 2004)

**Matilija Press**
**PMB 123**
**323 E. Matilija St., Ste. 110**
**Ojai, CA 93023**
**www.matilijapress.com**

# Disclaimer

This book was compiled and published as a reference for those interested in or involved in the writing and publishing process. It is not meant to be used in place of professional legal or financial advice and it comes with no guarantees of success. This book is a guide designed to help the writer, author and small publisher discover his/her own path to whatever measure and definition of success he or she might seek.

Since the publishing industry and the Internet are in a constant state of flux, we can't guarantee that the resources listed will always be current. It is our intention to offer you the most updated information available and to give you the tools to locate the additional resources you need.

# The Successful Writer's Handbook

## Table of Contents

# Book Reviewers' Pages

*The Successful Writer's Handbook* first emerged as an ebook. Booklocker.com thought highly enough of it to publish it on their site. Here are excerpts from some of the reviews generated as a result of that incarnation:

"This book can be an excellent tool for both the novice and the more advanced writer. Chapters are short, lucid and to the point. Good solid writing suggestions are offered for enabling the reader to understand what is needed if a successful writing career is in their future."
**Cindy Penn**
**WordWeaving**

"I highly recommend this book for those thinking about a writing career, for those looking to enhance their current writing business and for anyone who is interested in absorbing a professionally-written, well-organized piece of work that answers the basics and the essentials of writing as a career."
**Terri Mrosko, Publisher & Editor**
**Enhanced Communication Writing & Desktop Publishing Services**

"I found *The Successful Writer's Handbook* a well-written informative book filled with an abundance of excellent advice, facts and wisdom for the beginning and not so beginning writer. *The Successful Writer's Handbook* is one that I will keep in my own library."
**Molly Martin**
**Scribes World Reviews**

"Patricia Fry offers some great ideas on how to organize yourself and inch toward your dream of becoming a full time writer. The information is provided in a simple and lively manner which makes reading pleasurable. Overall, this surely is a complete handbook for any writer."
**Pooja Srinivas**
**Courses U Seek**

"Patricia Fry has written an excellent basic reference for writers who aspire to make a living from their work. And the book reads as though Patricia were giving you good advice across the kitchen table."
**Ron Litton**
**Ebook Reviews Weekly**

"Whether you're in love with writing but haven't begun to do it professionally or you've finished writing a novel and are waiting to get it published, you could find something useful in this book. It covers a wide range of areas in the field of writing from taking that first step towards being a freelance writer to writing a book and marketing it."
**Hasmita Chandler**
**Inscriptions Magazine**

"The keyword in the title of Patricia Fry's new book is 'successful.' She provides literally hundreds of suggestions for any writer from the beginner to published authors, to be successful."
**Peggy Hazelwood**
**Albooktross Electronic Bookstore**

"What distinguishes Patricia Fry from so many others in the business is her willingness to share her expertise and, more importantly, countless wonderful tips and strategies that are sure to benefit novice and seasoned writers alike. Writers at all levels and interests would be wise to invest in this well-crafted manual."
**Lori Joyal**
**Freelance Writer**

*"The Successful Writer's Handbook* is especially of value to the newer writer desiring a quick start in the business, or the writer who needs to jumpstart a career, but of help to everyone."
**Dana Cassell**
**Freelance Writer's Report**

# FOREWORD TO *The Successful Writer's Handbook*

Some people can write and some can teach. Few can do both well but Patricia Fry is an exception, as you will see when you read this book. I met Patricia (who I call Patty) over ten years ago, before I had written my first book, and I was immediately impressed by her creativity and professionalism. Everything she did, she appeared to do effortlessly. She was not only proficient, she was prolific. It wasn't until I got to know her that I realized she had struggled, as all successful authors do, to reach her goals.

Patty understood very early on in her writing career that there are sacrifices one must make to become a professional writer. She was willing to make them and they paid off handsomely for her. She has been a fulltime freelance writer now for three decades. Patty realized the importance of writing every day and she set aside time in her busy life to do so. She knew that it wasn't enough to be a good writer. To make a living at it, she had to be consistent, persistent, and knowledgeable about the magazine and book publishing industry.

In this book she shares her secrets of a successful career as a writer. Patty has not only written books and numerous articles having to do with writing, she has also written extensively on a variety subjects. Her advice is based on her own actual experience. She explains the many everyday details of a writing life such as creating your work place, organizing your work day, establishing a routine, keeping accurate records, and balancing your business and personal life. She emphasizes the importance of reliability and integrity. These are basic principles that you may never learn in a writing class but they are essential to the longevity of your professional writing career.

This book contains a wealth of information for any writer. You can pick it up, turn to any page, and find important information and answers to just about any question you may have. Even while Patty explains the work one must do to become a published writer, she herself is a shining example of the rewards. It is clear that Patty finds joy in her writing career and she teaches budding writers how they can, too.

**Mary Embree**
Literary Consultant and Author of *The Author's Toolkit: A Step-by-Step Guide to Writing and Publishing Your Book* (Allworth Press) and other nonfiction books

# Introduction

I've been writing for publication since 1973. I write articles for magazines such as, Writer's Digest, Canadian Author, Authorship, Columbia, The World and I, The Artist's Magazine, Your Health, Cat Fancy, Grit, Entrepreneur, Executive Update, Pages, Country Woman, ASPCA Animal Watch, The Walking Magazine, Woman's Own, Mature Outlook, Kiwanis, Teaching Tolerance,Guidepost, Country Business and Silicon 2.0.

I'm also the author of fifteen published books, including *A Writer's Guide to Magazine Articles for Book Promotion and Profit*, *Over 75 Good Ideas for Promoting Your Book* and *A Young Writer's Handbook*. I self-published these books and six others through my publishing company, Matilija Press (www.matilijapress.com).

For several years, I've written articles for the SPAWN newsletter and Web site. That's Small Publishers, Artists and Writers Network (www.spawn.org). I also write regularly for the National Association of Women Writers (www.naww.org). And my articles have been published by Albooktross, Author's Showcase, NovaLearn, Writers Review, Writing World, Writer's Insite, Writer's Weekly, Writing for Dollars, BookZone,Writer's Monthly and Freelance Writer's Report.

Each year, I respond to dozens of writers' questions for SPAWN and NAWW. And these questions have inspired numerous articles. This book features a collection of my best writing-related articles. Herein, you'll find the encouragement you'll need to start your writing career and the tools to make it work, such as: self-publishing how-tos and techniques, hundreds of tips for marketing your book, the nuts and bolts of operating your writing business and ideas for creating balance and harmony in your life.

- Do you know how to establish yourself as a writer?
- What are the pitfalls and benefits of being your own boss?
- How can you avoid writer's block?
- Can you make your book more salable before it's published?
- Where do writers find good article ideas?
- How do you write a book proposal?

- What should an author know about working with a publisher?
- How do you find niche markets?
- What should you strive for when posing for a publicity photo?
- Why do writers need other writers?
- How do you go about interviewing a high profile professional?
- What should a writer's Web site include?
- How can a writer take better care of him/herself?

You'll find answers to these and hundreds more questions in *The Successful Writer's Handbook*.

Start your educational journey now. Read this book from cover to cover, use the Table of Contents to pick and choose the topics you most want to review or rely upon the Index to find the information you need.

Happy reading and successful writing,
Patricia L. Fry

# *Chapter One*

...................

## *The Writing Life*

♦**Establish Yourself as a Writer**

♦**Parade Your Professional Persona**

♦**How to Find Work That Fulfills Your Passion**

♦**Coming Home to Write, How to Avoid the Pitfalls**

♦**Seven Rules for Crushing Writer's Block**

# Establish Yourself as a Writer

People often ask me, "How can I break into the writing profession?" Since this question cannot be answered in a paragraph or two, I've prepared this guide for those who are serious about establishing a writing career.

As I said in the introduction to this book, I've been writing for publication for thirty years. I've contributed hundreds of articles to about 175 different magazines and I have fifteen books to my credit. Writing is my full-time work. If you're thinking about designing a career around your love of writing either now or in the future, here's what I suggest:

- **Make a commitment**. I don't mean that you should give up your day job. On the contrary, it's wise to have an income to count on while you're testing the waters of this profession. If you're serious about a career as a freelance writer, however, take appropriate steps in that direction. Write every chance you get. Take on some writing assignments. You'll soon learn whether or not you're a self-starter, if you have organizational and time management skills and if you enjoy the work.

  My writing career was interrupted once by the necessity to work at a traditional job. I feared that full-time employment was in my future and that I would never be able to write seriously again. I became despondent. I had to prove to myself that I could write no matter what else was going on in my life. I started getting up everyday at 4 a.m. and I wrote for two hours before getting ready for work. I also wrote on weekends. I finished my book, *Quest for Truth*, in eight months on this schedule. Can you make this type of sacrifice and commitment?

- **Establish a routine and stick to it**. If you can't find the time to write, make some lifestyle changes. Give up some of your club and organization affiliations, stop watching so much television, get up an hour earlier, stay up later at night or cut back on your hours at work, for example. Log your daily activities to discover where you may be wasting time. Determine how much time you can devote to writing and schedule it.

- **Create a place to write.** Don't try to launch a writing career on the kitchen table where you share space with the family at mealtime. Set up permanent office space where the distractions are minimal—in a spare room or a corner of your bedroom, for example. (Read more about creating space to write on page 13.)

- **Practice self-discipline**. Lack of self-discipline is the cause of failure for many would-be writers. Here are three reliable disciplinary tactics for writers. Set strict hours and don't accept any excuses to deviate. Find a writing buddy—another writer with whom you can connect for support and encouragement. Reward yourself. Say, for example, "Once I finish this chapter, I'll take a thirty-minute walk." Or "As soon as I complete this brochure, I'll call a friend and chat for ten minutes." It may also be necessary to train friends and family to honor your working hours.

- **Become familiar with the markets**. Once you've established the area of writing you wish to pursue, spend time each week searching for potential clients. For example, study the magazines you want to write for, search out companies that contract writing work out or research possible publishers for your book. (Read more about finding work on page 9.)

- **Be a bold promoter.** It's well known that writers are usually more contented sitting at home quietly writing. In order to make a living as a writer, however, it's generally necessary to go out after the assignments. Design a marketing plan and pursue it. You'll find numerous ideas for putting your plan into action throughout this book.

- **Write, Write, Write**. Keep your mind and your fingers nimble by writing every single day.

The fact is that many people fail each year in their attempt to start a writing business. If you recognize yourself in the following list, refer to the seven tips above to pull yourself out of the quagmire.

Who is most likely to fail?

- **Those of little faith who don't even try.** I've heard people say that the writing field is saturated and that there's no room for anyone else. Writers who believe this will never experience their dream career.
- **Those who refuse to make sacrifices.**
- **Those who are too attached to their own writing.** While I don't advocate compromising your values, being a professional writer sometimes means making concessions. Be willing to rewrite your article at an editor's request. Agree to cut the number of words in your manuscript if it means landing a contract.
- **Those who can't step outside their comfort zone.** Everyone dislikes some aspect of his or her job. Writers, who are unwilling to perform certain tasks, such as conducting interviews and making cold calls, are limiting their usefulness, thus their marketability.

# Parade Your Professional Persona

Do you dream of earning your living as a writer? Maybe you're already getting paid for some of your short stories, articles or a self-published book. Perhaps you offer your writing or editing services to local businesses or individuals. If you receive payment for writing-related work, you are a working writer. But are you a professional writer? This depends on the quality of your work and how you conduct yourself with your clients, editors and publishers.

Writers, like artists, are notorious for being creative individuals without much of a business head. Most of us just want to write and to heck with all of those details associated with record keeping and relating to clients and editors. The fact is that if you want to supplement your income or earn a living through writing, you must enter the realm of business. The more writing you do for money, the more important your professional persona becomes.

**Maintain a professional manner**. While the world of business operates on a more casual level today, there are standards that separate a business conversation from an informal chat. There are differences between a chance meeting at the grocery store and a scheduled conference in your home office.

Preparation is key when conducting an interview for an article, negotiating a publishing contract or responding to a client's request for an accounting of your time, for example.

If you have children in the household or several family members who use the telephone, consider installing a business line that only you can answer. Connect it to an answering machine or voice mail for those times when you're not available. When you take a call on that line, make sure you come across sounding businesslike.

Appearances still make an impression. Dress appropriately for business meetings. Think about it, who would you hire to do detail oriented

writing work, someone who looks like they just threw on a pair o
sweats and a tee shirt they dug out of the dirty clothes hamper tha
morning or someone who dressed neatly for the occasion?

Likewise, when corresponding with a potential editor or client, use
proper grammar and, if you're not sure about your spelling, activate
spell check. I can't tell you how many emails I get from people who
claim they're writers, yet whose messages are riddled with misspelled
words and/or no or improper punctuation and capitalization. Trust me,
you won't be taken very seriously as a professional writer if your
presentation is sloppy.

**Be reliable**. Your willingness to follow through as promised will take
you a long way in your career. No matter what area of writing you
choose, you will be answering to someone else. It might be a publisher,
magazine editors, individual or business clients, distributors and
wholesalers or an agent, who will depend on you to fulfill a particular
obligation. A strong sense of responsibility will help you to succeed
and to excel in the writing business.

I've been writing articles for an association magazine for several years. I
always strive to produce a quality piece under deadline and according to
the editor's specifications. Four years ago, I earned a raise. And last year,
my diligence, reliability and efficiency paid off in an even bigger way. My
editor recommended me for a $3500 project with the International
organization and I landed the job. This would not have happened had I
been sloppy and lax in my dealings with the editor.

A couple of years ago, I agreed to write an article for a business
magazine. It wasn't the piece I pitched to them, but I gladly accepted
the assignment. I completed the article to their satisfaction and well
within their deadline. A few months later, they contacted me with
another assignment.

Earlier this year, an acquaintance invited me to submit a bid to rewrite
a simple brochure for a local public utility. The job took me three

hours and I charged accordingly. I also completed the work in a timely manner. A few months later, the board hired me to produce a 24-page booklet and write text for a large brochure—work that earned me a total of $4000.

It pays to make a good impression the first time and every time.

**Get organized**. To survive in any business, you have to know what's going on at every level: what publications are considering your articles? How many books have you sold in what arena? Who owes you money? Which clients could use more of your services?

I can't stress enough the importance of keeping good records. When a client asks for an accounting of your billed hours, you'd better have the records at your fingertips. If a bookstore owner calls and says he is going to ignore your invoice because he already paid for your last shipment of books, you need to have accurate records for reference.

Recently, an editor requested verification of the facts I used in an article on the dangers of a hot summer day. My organizational skills paid off. I was able to send him copies of data from my major sources.

Last month, I had to contact an editor about payment for an article. His secretary said she had already sent me a check. My records indicated, however, that the check they sent me was for the article they had published the month before. They still owed me for the piece they ran during the month in question. I explained this to them and received payment a few days later.

It's easy to get rattled or even a bit defensive when discussing a late payment, a problem with a rewrite or a discrepancy about billable hours. That's why I recommend maintaining your professional composure on such occasions by putting time and space between yourself and the individual with whom there's an issue. Say, for example, "Let me check on that and I'll call you back." After you've had a chance to review the details of the transaction, make notes and return the call with confidence and facts. If there's still a problem, calmly offer to send copies of you records and ask to see theirs. Most disparities can be resolved fairly.

It's not difficult to maintain a professional image. It just takes a little forethought and planning. Observe other people at work. Who do you like doing business with? Most likely it's someone who's reliable courteous, trustworthy and prompt. Embrace the professional qualities that you admire and you, too, will be thought of as a professional.

# How to Find Work That Fulfills Your Passion

As president of SPAWN (Small Publishers, Artists and Writers Network) and a regular contributor to the National Association of Women Writers (NAWW) newsletter and Web site, I also respond to writers' questions for both organizations. One of the most frequently asked questions relates to finding writing work.

For example, Lydia wrote, "My dream is to quit my job and become a full-time writer. Can you tell me how to get started?"

Jon asked, "What does it take to become a freelance writer? I'm disabled and want to do this work from my home."

Rachel writes, "I'm a college graduate with a degree in journalism, but I can't find work. Can you give me some job search advice?"

Whether you're looking for corporate work, want to write for a newspaper or yearn to do freelance writing or editing, the opportunities are plentiful. If you can construct a sentence and you're willing to approach job hunting with gusto, an open mind and a lot of creativity, you will find work.

Here's my checklist for job hunters:

## General Advice

- **Subscribe to online writing-oriented newsletters** and join online writing organizations that offer job listings for writers. Many of them also keep you current on publishing trends. Here are a couple of resources to get you started: The Write Jobs (www.writerswrite.com/jobs), WriterFind (www.writerfind.com), SPAWN (www.spawn.org), NAWW (www.naww.org) and Writer's Weekly (www.writersweekly.com).

- **Network constantly**. Attend writers/publishers' events and ask people how they got their jobs/assignments. Find local writers organizations through your library, bookstores and in the calendar section of the newspaper. Participate in interactive Web sites for writers. Locate online sites using your favorite search engine. Type in "writers groups" or "writer," for example. I found a potential publisher for a client's book recently while networking with a fellow writer. Last year, a writer friend suggested I contact an editor she knows about trying my hand at technical writing. I ended up writing a dozen articles for this magazine during a twelve-month period. (Read more about networking on page 122.)

- **Volunteer your writing services**. A little volunteer work might land you the job you seek. Offer to write the church bulletin, a company newsletter or a press release for a charity organization. Not only are you gaining experience and adding to your portfolio, you're showing off your talent and skills to all of the right people.

- **Read the classified employment ads** and apply for every job that has "writing" in it. Post your resume on some of the major Internet recruiting sites such as monster.com. And search their databases for job opportunities.

- **Create a portfolio** and keep adding to it. Make copies of your published articles, brochures, etc. to show prospective employers/clients.

- **Build a Web site** and post your portfolio and resume there. (Read more about a writer's Web site on page 149.)

- **Keep writing.** Write every chance you get. Practice, practice, practice.

- **Be open** to all types of writing. You may have your heart set on becoming rich and famous writing a novel or landing a job as the editor-in-chief of *Reader's Digest*. In the meantime, however, accept the work that comes your way. Do some PR writing for your neighbor, ghost write a book for a client or proof a friend's manuscript. Get paid and learn new skills.

## If You Want a Writing Job in the Corporate World

- **Study the materials from companies** for which you'd like to work and see if you can improve upon them. Show your ideas to the appropriate department head.

- **Join business organizations** and service clubs where you can network with businessmen and women who might hire someone with your skills.

- **Sign with a temp agency** as a writer. This may be your foot-in-the-door.

## If You're Hoping for a Job With a Major Newspaper

- **Hire on at a small newspaper** while waiting for your big break. There's an ongoing turnover at newspapers, so they're always hiring. This is not a glamorous job, but it's a step in the right direction. I got my first job writing a business column for a local newspaper.

- **Cover a story on speculation** for the newspaper of your choice. Watch for the opportunity to write about a local issue and offer it to the newspaper for a fee. Attend meetings and events that aren't being covered by the news staff and offer to report on them. Your effort is bound to get the editor's attention.

## Create Your Own Work

- **Write articles for magazines**. For this profession, you'll need writing, organizational and research skills as well as patience and a great deal of self-discipline. You'll also need the following tools: a computer, *Writer's Market* (a reference book for writers found in the reference section of most libraries and bookstores) and *A Writer's Guide to Magazine Articles for Book Promotion and Profit* (Matilija Press, www.matilijapress.com). (Read more about article writing on page 20.)

- **Become an editor**. Start by approaching busy freelance editors and see if they need help accommodating their clients. The editors I know often turn clients away because they're too busy.

<u>**Help Yourself**</u>
- **Find a mentor**—someone who will guide you through the steps to building your writing business

- **Don't give up your day job**. If you need the money and can't keep waiting for *the* job to come along, go to work and write in your spare time. "What spare time?" you might ask. This may be one of those situations where you have to make some sacrifices

Use this checklist to generate other ideas. The point is to keep on keeping on. My writer friend, Kathy, earns a living for herself and two sons writing technical manuals. After struggling long and hard to find this job, she advises other writers, "You can't win if you don't play."

# Coming Home to Write
# How to Avoid the Pitfalls

You've finally made the decision to become a full-time writer. Perhaps your youngest child enters school this year. Maybe you've taken early retirement or you quit your job and now you're going to pursue your dream to write. Life is wonderful! Or is it?

If you're like many beginning freelancers, you're not quite sure how to begin. You're trying to work from home now and it's a virtual hub of activity. There are dishes to wash, lawns to mow, beds to make, a refrigerator full of food calling to you, dogs barking and possibly children underfoot. How do you discipline yourself to work amidst these household distractions?

After years of practice, I've established some home-business standards. Here they are:

**1: Arrange separate office space**. Don't try to embark upon a writing career in the hub of the household. You need a separate and permanent place to write. Ideally, you can transform a spare room into an office. Even a closet might suffice as an office for a time. Don't laugh. I once had a sewing room in a closet. Build a desk, install a good light fixture and electrical outlets and pull up a chair. One writer I know had a cubical constructed in her garage to use as an office. A little insulation, a piece of carpeting, a space heater and some colorful posters made her feel right at home and cozy there.

**2: Set strict business hours**. Commit to even two or three hours per day at first, while you're acclimating yourself to this way of working. As soon as you can, shift into a six or eight-hour workday. You might start work at 8 a.m., take thirty minutes for lunch and then continue working until 4:30. If you have young children coming home from school at 2:30, work from 8 – 2. I go to work at 5 every morning and quit around 5 p.m. I take about two hours off throughout the day to walk, water my garden and run errands.

If you're accustomed to having someone else structure your workday or if you've been operating life without a schedule, put your business hours in writing. Make a sign stating these hours and post it on your office door. Block out this time on your engagement calendar.

If you're easily distracted by household chores or hobbies, schedule time on your calendar for these activities as well. Knowing that you can look forward to time off to do other things, will help you to focus on work during working hours.

**3: Organize your time**. Most freelance writers have a variety of responsibilities to handle each day and sometimes coordinating these tasks can be overwhelming. Over the years, I've discovered that I spend approximately two-thirds of my time writing, editing, proofreading, doing research and conducting interviews. The rest of my time is spent promoting books and new article ideas, working with distributors and tasks related to bookkeeping. When I'm working with clients, the ratio is similar (two-thirds of my time on client work and one-third drumming up new business and taking care of details).

It makes sense to plan your day/week/month accordingly. Of course, the reason you're in this business is for the joy of writing. But if you spend four days during the week writing, you'd better devote one day to making new business contacts and another day chasing down money owed, reading contracts, logging transactions and so forth. If you don't take care of the details of your business, you don't really have a business.

Likewise, organize your time away from home. Rather than running errands several times a week, save them up to do all at once. I keep a running list. When I go out, I might do a little library research, deliver books to a local bookstore, buy supplies, conduct an interview, pick up some photos for an article and ship some books.

**4: Prioritize.** When you're your own boss, sensible prioritization is vital to your success. Following through with a client's project becomes more important than cleaning house, for example. Often more difficult is deciding which business tasks to handle in what order. I know many writers who spend a lot of time spinning their wheels instead of being productive because they can't determine their priorities.

Here are my criteria: Let's say that I have three articles to write. I'll generally work on the article for the highest paying magazine first, or the one for an editor who sends a lot of work my way. If the lower paying magazine has the closest deadline, I'll typically finish that one first, making sure to leave plenty of time to complete the others within their deadlines.

If I have an article to write, a request for rewrites on a book manuscript for a publisher and a book proposal to compile for a client, I'll work on the project with the closest deadline. If there are no deadlines, I might schedule time each day for each project so no one has to wait long for the finished product.

**5: Learn to deal with distractions**. Another real problem for many freelance writers are the distractions that normally occur around the home. There are household tasks waiting to be tackled, barking dogs, neighbors stopping by, personal telephone calls and sometimes children under foot. Most writers can successfully minimize personal interruptions with honesty and bribery. Friends and family may find it difficult to take you seriously as a writer at first. It's up to you to demonstrate your professionalism and sometimes you might have to be rather firm.

Learn to say "no." I like to offer something when I take something away. For example, when a friend calls to invite you to lunch, say, "I'd love to go, but I'm working on a deadline this week. Can we go after church on Sunday? Or how about coming over here for dinner next Thursday evening?"

I know several women and a couple of men who juggle parenthood and writing. One mother says, "I write while my three-year-old is sleeping. I also have a little corner in my office where Justin can play while I'm working. He has his own desk with a toy computer, play telephone, paper, colored markers and so forth. Sometimes he'll entertain himself for nearly an hour at a time. And I've had to learn to get a lot of work done during short intervals."

**6: Adopt rituals.** Two major problems for the dozens of home-based workers I've interviewed over the years are, how to start working each day and how to quit. I suggest adopting rituals.

For me, squeezing a glass of fresh orange juice and starting the coffee, are my cues to go to work. A friend of mine doesn't start working until after she has a cup of coffee and reads the morning newspaper. I interviewed a graphic artist once who leaves his home every morning around 7, enjoys a cup of coffee downtown and then comes back home to work. He says, this is the ritual that works for him.

Many writers find it easier to start working in the morning when they're not facing a blank screen. I like to leave something unfinished at quitting time, so I can ease into my work routine the next day.

As for rituals to help you quit working, turn off the computer at 5 o'clock, close your office door, plan specific activities for yourself or with the family during the evening so you won't be tempted to go to work out of boredom. One writer says, "Putting everything away helps me to officially close the office for the day."

**7: Create a healthy balance.** It's up to you to establish your personal and business lifestyle and pace. When developing a schedule around your work, be sure to include outdoor activities, mental stimulation, social events, time with friends/family, creative hobbies, physical activity and a spiritual component. Remember, in order to do your best at work, you need to participate in play. For additional encouragement, read The Care and Feeding of the Whole Writer on page 170.

# Seven Rules for Crushing Writer's Block

It's more than annoying. It can be downright debilitating to find yourself sitting in front of the computer staring at a blank screen. Your deadline is looming and you can't think of anything to write. You wonder if you'll ever pen another word. Writer's Block is frustrating, but it's not fatal, nor is it usually permanent.

I'm often asked if I ever suffer from Writer's Block. And I have to say, "No." But that's only because I know how to overcome it. Here are some remedies that work for me.

**Just start writing**. No, I'm not trying to be a wise guy. I can't count the number of times an article has begun to take shape after I started typing even unrelated words on the blank screen. Don't wait hours, days or years for inspiration. Go ahead and type your name, address and phone number in the upper left corner of the screen. Type out some ideas for a title. And then just start pouring out random thoughts on the subject of your story or article. Let the words flow without editing. You'll be surprised at how quickly your story will begin to develop.

**Use another method of writing**. When the words won't come, I sometimes find it helpful to get away from the computer and sit down with my favorite pen and pad. While I still may not be able to write the first sentence, I generally come up with several great ideas for the article. And once I transfer those ideas to the computer, the article starts to take shape.

**Write something else**. One of the benefits of being a writer is that we never run out of things to write about. Right? When I truly can't get into a particular assignment, I switch to another one. If you're feeling too chipper to write the murder scene for your novel, for example, move on to the party chapter. If you're stuck on a piece about ergonomics in the workplace, put it aside and spend this time on your story about the history of the teddy bear.

**Get involved in a different task.** As a full-time freelance writer, I have a constant array of tasks to do every week. If I don't feel like tackling a particular project, I can choose another one. I might decide to conduct an interview, clean out one of my filing cabinets, send query letters, write new marketing material for one of my books or start the research for another article.

**Boost your ego.** Sometimes Writer's Block can bruise one's self esteem. In this case, it's wise to do something to increase your confidence level. If you excel in the kitchen, go bake one of your most creative desserts. If you have a knack with watercolors, paint for thirty minutes. It's easier to break through Writer's Block when you feel good about yourself.

**Get active.** Fresh air and exercise are extremely freeing and healing for someone with Writer's Block. Get out and walk, jog, bicycle, garden, swim or fly a kite. You'll go back to work with a new perspective on your story.

**Meditate**. Often Writer's Block is nothing more than a temporary lack of concentration. Writers typically feel blocked when they're stressed or rushing to meet a deadline, for example. Whenever I feel overwhelmed and I can't focus on the writing assignment at hand, I meditate. I close my eyes and sit quietly for a few minutes. I clear my mind of the clutter from the day. And I ask for clarity and focus. If meditation isn't your stress-reliever of choice, write in your journal for fifteen minutes, read something inspirational or pray. You might be surprised at what you can accomplish when you consciously release the stresses of the day.

## *Chapter Two*

..............................

### *Get Ready, Get Set, Write!*

♦Seven Steps to Getting Your Articles Published

♦Query Etiquette and Expertise

♦Where Oh Where Are All the Good Articles Ideas?

♦The Anatomy of an Article

♦Recycle and Profit

# Seven Steps to Getting Your Articles Published

Do you have an idea or two that you want to develop into articles? Would you like to earn your living writing articles for magazines? I used to dream of seeing my articles published in a variety of national magazines. My dream came true and so can yours. Here's how to get started:

### Research the market.

Study the magazines for which you want to write. What type of articles do they publish? What is the writing style? Can you define the tone of the articles? Do they publish essays, first-person accounts, bulleted pieces, profiles or in-depth articles that require interviews and research? Even the letters-to-the-editor and the ads will reveal something about the readership, thus the type of articles and stories the magazine can use.

If you are attached to a particular type of writing, you may have to research through the backdoor. In other words, locate magazines that use the type of articles you write. Don't waste time sending your essays or personal experience article to a publication that prints only well-researched, educational articles. Avoid bothering the editor of a how-to crafts magazine with your rendition of "My Memories of Sewing With Mama."

### List your article ideas.

Start with familiar topics. Study the listings in *Writer's Market* to come up with more ideas. *They* say, as a beginner, you should write about what you know. I endorse this recommendation. If you're the mother of twins or triplets, consider writing for a parenting magazine or a publication that celebrates multiple birth families. Maybe you're a pilot. Start by writing something for aviation or in-flight magazines. When I started writing, my family was involved with horses. The first several articles I sold related to this hobby. Among my other interests that have fostered articles are writing and publishing, growing African violets, public speaking, cats, youth mentoring, grandparenting, walking for exercise and gardening.

### Determine your slant.

You're probably filled with good ideas for article topics. The difficult part is determining your slant. Of course, this will depend on the magazine that you're pitching. Let's use the African violet topic as an example. I sold several articles on starting violets from leaves and growing healthy African violets to a variety of home and garden, women's, country, rural and regional magazines. A farming association magazine bought my piece featuring a Colorado woman who grew commercial African violets at home. My public speaking articles have appeared in business, writing, association and women's magazines. And I've sold articles on walking and meditation walking to health, religious, regional, women's and general publications.

## Write a query letter.

Although some magazine editors ask for the complete manuscript, most want to see a query letter. A query letter typically introduces you and pitches your idea. On your letterhead, include the date, a brief synopsis of the article, names of the experts you plan to interview, your qualifications to write this article and your writing credits. Keep your letter to one page if at all possible. Send your query letter to more than one editor simultaneously. If you're sending it by regular mail, always enclose a self-addressed-stamped envelope (SASE). More and more editors request queries by email today. But certainly not all of them. Some editors have a strong dislike for email and will delete query letters without reading them. (Learn more about query letters on page 23.)

## Write the article.

Once you get the go-ahead from an editor, note their required word count and deadline. Write the article to their specifications. Do they want a 900-word profile piece or a 1200-word how-to? It's easy to agonize at this point. You wonder, "Will the editor like this catchy phrase or should I eliminate it?" "Will he/she appreciate my attempt at humor, or will they hate it?" I've found it best to just write as closely to their specifications as possible, using a recent copy of their magazine as a guide. One of three things will happen: They will reject it and you'll probably never know why. They will accept it as is. Or they will ask for a rewrite.

## Recycle your article.

Once you've sold an article on a favorite topic, write another one or two or three. If you sold first or one-time rights to a previously published article, you can submit it to a new magazine. Check the listings in *Writer's*

*Market* for magazines that publish reprints and/or request Writer's Guidelines from the magazines for which you want to write. (Read more about recycling your articles on page 33.)

**Keep good records.**

Create a record of each query letter and article you send. Log all activity related to each article. An efficient record-keeping system will help in your communications with editors. Also, keep track of expenses and payments. (Read more about bookkeeping for writers on page 140.)

# Query Etiquette and Expertise

If you want to get published, you have to make a good first impression when approaching an editor or publisher. How? Write a good—no, write a *great* query letter.

Why is the query letter so important? It saves everyone a lot of time. Editors are more likely to look at a one-page letter than an entire manuscript. And you don't have to write the piece until you know there's an interest. Often, an editor will suggest changes to your initial idea. This is easy to manage if the article is still in idea form. If the article is already written, you'll have to do a rewrite.

For example, two years ago, I queried *Technology and Learning Magazine* about an article on preparing girls for careers in technology. Instead, the editors asked me to write about public relations programs in American schools. I recently offered to write an article for *Children's Voice* highlighting the healing powers of gardening for at-risk children. The editor saw more merit in a piece featuring specific gardening programs for kids, however. These are only a few examples showing the benefits of querying first.

Before even thinking about writing that query letter, request a copy of the magazine and the publisher's Guidelines for Writers— sometimes available at the Web site.

While there is plenty of room for creativity when writing a query letter, there are also certain standards. Following is the anatomy of a query letter:

1: **Date your letter and address it to the appropriate editor**. If the source you're using for contact information is over six-months old, I suggest confirming the information. How?
- Look at the masthead in a current issue of the magazine.
- Send an email or call to verify the contact information.
- Check their Web site, but make sure their data has been updated recently.

2: **State your intent**. Identify your correspondence as a query letter. I typically write, "I'd like to propose an article featuring…" Or I might start my letter with an attention-getting statement. Here's an example: "Do people often interrupt you when you're talking? Are your comments sometimes ignored? Do you feel inadequate when expressing your ideas in a business meeting? In a recent survey, over fifty-percent of the women polled said they do not feel that they're taken seriously at work. If you're one of these women, my article, 'Be Heard: How to Get People to Listen When You Speak' could change your life."

3: **Write a synopsis of your proposed article or book**. Briefly and succinctly describe your story and your slant. Introduce your experts and/or supply a list of research sources and one or two sample anecdotes you plan to use. Avoid inundating the editor with details, but don't play guessing games, either. Be straightforward in your presentation. Give the editor everything she needs in order to make her decision while keeping the synopsis portion within a paragraph or two.

4: **Demonstrate that you've done your homework**. Hopefully, your article or book idea is on target for the magazine or publisher you've contacted. That's the first indication that you've done adequate research. If you believe your article is a good fit for a particular column, mention it. Also, state your proposed word count based on their guidelines.

5: **List your qualifications.** If you have a particular proficiency or experience related to your proposed topic, mention it. In a query letter for an article about writing, I will state that I've been writing for publication for thirty years and I'll refer to my experience related to the topic. When querying for an article about helping instead of criticizing neighborhood kids, I write about my affiliation with a youth mentoring organization and a Neighborhood Watch program.

6: **Give your writing credits**. This is no time to be modest. List your most significant and pertinent works. If you've sold anything similar to this topic, say so. If you're hard-pressed to come up with appropriate writing credits, go ahead and mention your work on the church newsletter or the fact that you're a fourth grade teacher. Send a couple of published clips, if available.

7: **End it**. I generally close with something like, "Please let me know if you're interested." In the case of a rather complicated piece, I might say, "If you'd like to see a more detailed outline (or a book proposal), please let me know."

8: **Keep things simple.** Make it easy for the editor to work with you. First, find out how the editor prefers that you send your letter—regular mail, email or fax. This information generally appears in their Guidelines for Writers. Send just what the editor requests (a query letter and three published clips, for example). If he or she wants more, they'll ask.

Like many writers, I have a Web site. At the end of my query letter, I often add my Web site address and write after it, "for more about me" or "to view my published articles."

Keep your query letter to one page if at all possible. I've been known to spill over to a page and a half when I have several experts and research sources to list. That's forgivable.

Additional tips (and these are important, too):
- Neatness counts.
- Always include a self-address-stamped envelope (SASE).
- Log every transaction. List date sent, magazine/publisher name and article/book description. Leave a space to record any notes.

### The Waiting Game
Expect to wait a while before receiving a reply. The waiting period could last anywhere from three day to three months after sending a query letter by mail. The average is probably four to six weeks. Email has changed the waiting period to some degree. Before using email, make sure this is okay with the editor. While some editors adore this mode of communication, others will not look at anything that isn't sealed in an envelope.

I like to use email because generally, an editor will respond more swiftly. As with regular mail, however, there are some editors and publishers that you will not hear from. My records indicate that nearly one-third of the query letters I sent last year were ignored. It's frustrating, isn't it? And the waiting game can be most annoying.

New writers, especially, often lose patience with editors who take their time to respond. One way around this discomfort is to avoid putting all of your hopes and dreams on that one query letter.

I don't wait for query responses anymore because I'm too busy sending out new queries. Send your query to more than one editor. Write new queries on different topics. Be productive and you won't get stuck in wait mode

You may wonder:

How long should I wait for a response?
- Wait at least four to six weeks before inquiring about a query or an unsolicited manuscript. Then send a tracer letter stating, "According to my records, on January 12, 2002, I queried you about an article featuring techniques for attracting birds to your patio garden. I'm writing now to inquire as to the status of that idea." I've sold several articles by following up like this. Editors misplace letters. Sometimes queries are never received. Often, I'm asked to resubmit the piece. Some editors pay more attention to a letter or manuscript the second time around.

What shall I do while I'm waiting for a response?
- Send your query to other magazines and write new query letters. Set goals. Send a query on a new topic every day or submit three queries per week. I send between thirty and fifty queries each month. And I receive between 8 and 12 article assignments.

For those of you who are still a little overwhelmed by the idea of writing a query letter, I've devised this guide. Ask yourself the following questions to help you write that query.

1. To whom shall I address this query?
2. What type of material is this publication requesting? (How-to articles, essays, inspirational pieces…?)
3. What type of article or story do I have to offer them that might meet their current needs?
4. What aspect of my idea will appeal to them most?
5. How can I let the editor know that I'm familiar with his publication/ publishing company?
6. How can I convince the editor/publisher that I can create a good and credible story from this topic?
7. How can I convince the editor/publisher that I am the person to write this piece?
8. What can I do to make it easy for the editor/publisher to work with me?

# Where Oh Where Are All the Good Article Ideas?

Having contributed hundreds of articles to numerous magazines on a variety of topics, I'm often asked, "Where do you get your article ideas?" I say, "Look everywhere." Here's a guide to get you started:

**Write About What You Know**
What skills do you have? What are your interests and hobbies? What insights have you gained over the years? Create article ideas from your own personal knowledge and talents.

I mentioned in an earlier Chapter that, when I started my writing career, we were involved in horses as a family and, in fact, we subscribed to several horse-related magazines. I studied those magazines from cover to cover and fairly quickly came up with some article ideas. Consequently, I sold dozens of articles to horse magazines. As an example, my first article featured various ways to use your horse show ribbons. I sold another one on creative and practical hairdos for horse shows. And I placed a humorous piece about being a horse show mother.

**Write About Things You Want to Know**
A good way to learn about something is to write about it. I once wrote a piece on chain letters because I wanted to know more about the concept and whether or not it could work. In order to write an in depth article, you have to do the research, right?

I've also written about the dangers in a hot summer day, the dynamics of a habit, how men and women are using intuition in the work place and cat personalities—all because I wanted to learn more about these topics.

**Share Your Experiences**
Each of us has unique experiences. Use yours to develop good articles. I've sold articles based on my experiences with caring for an aging horse, rescuing feral kittens, helping to build a safer neighborhood, long-distance grandparenting and working at home, for example. I also wrote a book profiling my experiences working with a hypnotherapist who used past life regression therapy. Someday I hope

to write stories about our family horse packing trips into the wilderness. Of course it's fashionable, right now, to write your memoirs.

## Relate the Experiences of Others
Make money by tapping into the life adventures of family, friends and acquaintances. Get their permission, of course. Most people love to see their names in print and are willing to be interviewed. I've sold stories about the perilous experience of a rider whose horse went over a cliff and lived, a youngster who started an adopt-a-grave program to save a neglected pioneer cemetery, a traveling farrier, a man who invented a new type of gun lock and many articles profiling people in interesting or successful businesses. One writer I know wrote a book about the experiences of her friend, a World War II Veteran.

## Look Everywhere For Article Ideas
I once met a woman in line at the post office who did home repairs and renovation. This chance meeting resulted in a couple of published articles. My long distance grandparenting book came about while shopping at the grocery store. I overheard two women talking about how difficult it is to bond with grandchildren who live miles away. While most people complain about standing in line and grocery shopping, I consider these opportunities.

I've also found article ideas at my grandsons' Little League games, at a Neighborhood Watch meeting, while traveling and during a family reunion.

## Stop, Look and Listen
Pay attention to the world around you. Notice what people are doing and listen to what they're saying. Other people are excellent resources for a writer whether you write nonfiction or fiction.

I heard a young mother complain recently that her family rarely sits down and shares a meal together. This prompted me to write a piece on how to bring the family back to the supper table. A friend told me one day that she had met a man online. So I wrote an article about computer dating. After sitting through a poorly executed presentation, I went home and wrote an article on effective public speaking.

## Keep Up With the News

Your newspaper is brimming with article ideas. Read it everyday from cover to cover. This is how I came up with the idea for an article on healing and therapeutic gardens and gardening. I also got the idea for a piece featuring cats in the workplace from the newspaper. And my 3500-word article on innovative PE programs came about after reading a short article on the growing trend toward obesity in children.

## Use the Internet

Open up to new topics that you come across while Web surfing. I do a lot of Internet research and often discover potential article ideas while on my way to do something else. My piece on Internet recruiting developed from an unrelated Internet research project. My article on raising a better student came about after a chance Web site visit. And it was a Web search that led to my article featuring Internet sites for the cat owner

## Write From the Heart

What are you passionate about? How would you like to make a difference? I've written articles on teaching kids responsibility through horse ownership, youth mentoring and how America is helping our children.

As you can see, coming up with article ideas is as easy as paying attention to the world around you. Oh, that gives me an idea for an article on how to sharpen your observation skills.

# The Anatomy of an Article

Many eager writers develop their first few articles based mainly on what they want to say. They have a story to tell, a point to make or a gripe to air, and they do so with little regard for the reader.

It's wonderful to be dedicated to your topic, but it's also important to connect with your audience. If your article or story isn't presented in an organized manner, readers will not receive your message.

The logical order of an article involves a beginning, a middle and an end.

1: THE BEGINNING. There are a number of ways to start your article. Begin with an introduction, make an announcement or open with a provocative statement. The primary purpose is to pique the reader's interest. Say, for example, "Sweating makes you healthier." Readers will certainly want to know how this is possible. Or start with an anecdote, " Sarah Lynn Rivers used to average a cold every six months. Two years ago, she started power walking and she hasn't had so much as a sniffle since." I would certainly be eager to read on.

2: THE MIDDLE. I tend to break the middle of my articles into thirds— the first third ties in with the beginning and serves to explain the purpose of the article. In this case, your intent might be to explore and explain the benefits of regular physical exercise. The second third should take your readers to the main points of the piece. Using statistics, anecdotes and quotes, outline the benefits of exercise. The last third might involve suggestions for how the reader can design his/her own exercise program.

3: THE ENDING. A technique that generally works, is to bring your article full circle. Say, for example, "So get out there and sweat for your health" or "If you're missing work because of frequent colds, get out in the fresh air and start walking your way to health."

Additional tips:
**Make smooth transitions**. A transition is a bridge from one thought or idea to another. For example, "Not only does regular exercise ward off

the common cold, it has been proven to keep more serious ailments at bay." After substantiating this statement with statistics, anecdotes and expert quotes, you might write, "The exercise habit is also beneficial to your sense of well-being. How? It can ensure a more restful night's sleep, increase your energy level and even put you in a better mood."

**Stay in the same tense and person**. An article usually represents the present and is often written in the second person. In this case, you will use statements such as, "Exercise is good for you." Anecdotes and examples may take you temporarily into another tense and person, and this is okay. Don't, however, shift from *you* to *they* to *we* in an article without reason.

**Add variety**. Create a more interesting article by using a mixture of narrative, anecdotes, quotes and statistics. A few years ago, someone sent me an article to critique. The writer chose a first person essay style for a piece on raising chinchillas. A few examples, anecdotes and expert quotes changed this from a dry narrative to a more lively and interesting article.

There's no great mystery to writing a good article. It just takes planning, logic, organization and creativity.

# Recycle and Profit

If you write articles for magazines, you probably average between $200 and $600 per article that you sell. How would you like to double, triple or even quadruple that figure? You can. All you have to do is recycle your articles. Think about it, if one editor finds your article worthy of publication, others likely will, too.

There are basically two ways to recycle an article. Offer it as a reprint—sell the same article over and over again. Or rewrite the piece with a different audience in mind.

How lucrative is the article recycling business? Nearly one-third of the articles I sold last year were either reprints or rewrites. And some of these second-hand articles earned more than the original piece.

I once wrote a feature on how to help a friend through the grieving process. Not only did I resell the original article a number of times, I used the initial research to write pieces on helping children grieve, for a parenting magazine; how to give and receive emotional support, for a religious magazine and tips for mourning the death of a relationship, for a woman's magazine. I even stretched the theme to include an article exploring the emotions in business for an entrepreneurial magazine.

My article featuring how to live successfully alone was first published in *Columbia Magazine.* Subsequent reprints and rewrites netted me nearly $4500 over the next couple of years. I developed this idea to include articles on how to be single in America, how to survive the holidays alone and issues around the empty nest syndrome, for example.

Grandparenting is one of my most lucrative topics. I've generated over $6500 from approximately two dozen articles covering such topics as, traveling with grandkids, choosing gifts for grandchildren, how to teach grandkids money awareness, how to bond with your new grandbaby, grandparent/grandchild activities and so forth

Is recycling worthwhile? As you can see, I would have missed out on $11,000 in total income if I'd stopped with one article to one publication in just these two categories.

Following are additional ideas to help you on your road to recycling success.

**Retain your rights.** The potential for additional income is just one good reason to retain the rights when you sell your work. If you want to resell an article as a reprint, you must own the rights to that article. This means that you'll want to offer one-time rights or first rights when you sell the original article. If you inadvertently give up your rights to an article (sell all-rights to the piece), you can still rewrite it and offer it to a non-competing publication.

Note: some magazines that request all rights will revert limited rights back to you after publication. Likewise, sometimes you can alter an all-rights contract to read, "one-time rights" or "first rights." Contracts are not etched in stone and are often negotiable.

**Keep a reprint log.** While seeking a publisher for your original article idea, also note which publications are good candidates for a reprint on this topic. This list will save you a lot of time when you're ready to send out reprints.

**Represent your reprint as a reprint**. Make sure the editor knows that you're offering him/her a previously published article. The obvious way to do this is to send a copy of the published clip via regular mail. We're more inclined today, however, to use email. So how does one distinguish the difference between an original article and a reprint?

I note on the first page of my manuscript that I'm offering reprint rights and where and when the article was first published. Whether you send your reprint via the postal service or email, always include a cover letter. State that the enclosed is a reprint and where/when it was first published.

## Actively market your reprints

Anytime I send a query letter or a reprint, I also enclose a list of some of my former article topics. This has proven to be an excellent marketing tool for my writing business. Maybe the editor isn't in the market for an article on the subject of my query or reprint, but is wildly interested in a piece featuring a topic from my list.

**Recycle your good ideas.** Once you've sold an article on an important subject or a favorite topic, write another one or two or three. Here are some ideas from my own files:

I once wrote an article for a religious family magazine featuring family togetherness. The following articles developed from that idea:

> Family camping activities
> Spiritual activities for families
> Togetherness ideas for the busy family
> Family togetherness through exercise
> How your computer can enhance family togetherness
> How to collect your family history

I wrote an article for a general magazine on how to teach your child responsibility. That one developed into articles on:

> Teaching your child the work ethic
> Teaching children money awareness
> Teaching children responsibility through pet ownership
> Encouraging a child's independence
> The corporate sector's involvement in preparing children for the workplace

My 3500-word piece on healing and therapeutic gardens for *The World and I Magazine* fostered additional articles on:

> Meditation and contemplation gardens
> Gardens that heal children
> The walking garden

**How much can you charge?** Magazines typically pay anywhere from $25 to $500 for a reprint. Most pay half or three-quarters of what they pay for an original article.

Sometimes, however, you can sell a recycled idea or a reprint for more than you were paid for the original. Recently, I wrote a piece for a general magazine featuring two teenaged brothers who had written a book to help children cope with diabetes. A few months later, I rewrote this story for a family magazine and they paid me five times the amount the first magazine paid.

Years ago I wrote an article on how to handle the irate customer. I sold it few times in various incarnations for various purposes for a total of about $800. Then an association magazine contacted me about running a reprint in their publication for $1200.

I've even sold articles on the same subject to competing magazines by changing the slant. Again, my grandparenting topic is a good example of this. *Columbia* bought my article on long-distance grandparenting. *Catholic Forester* commissioned my piece illustrating how specific grandparents and grandchildren relate to one another. And *St. Anthony Messenger* purchased my article on how to be a more effective grandparent in today's changing world.

**Keep accurate records.** As part of your bookkeeping system, note the rights you've sold with each article and whether the article is an original or a reprint.

**Get organized**. Probably one of the most difficult aspects of this freelance business is defining the term, "good use of time." Writers struggle constantly to establish a working routine that actually works. The schedule they designed last week, becomes suddenly obsolete. That said, I strongly urge you to set aside time at least once a month to send out reprints and to develop new ideas around some of your old articles.

Don't rest on your laurels after having one magnificent piece published. With little time and effort, you can recycle and profit.

## Chapter Three

..................................

*How to Write for Niche Markets*

♦Discovering Your Niche

♦Local History, a Lucrative Niche Market

♦Writing Close to Home

♦Write for the Regionals

♦Write About Where You've Been

# Discovering Your Niche

While some writers discover their niche early in their career, others struggle to find their rightful place. In fact writers can be divided into two types. There are those who have a specialty or a specific area of knowledge they want to share and those who have no particular expertise, but who just want to write.

A writer with a specialty is not necessarily interested in writing for the sake of writing. He or she has something to say—a message to share—and writing happens to be a popular method of spreading the word. Thus, a psychologist might write a book on taming ADD in kids without medication and he takes his book on tour to raise awareness. The animal rights activist writes articles purely to gain recognition for her cause. The high-profile attorney writes a book about his most notorious case in order to attain celebrity status. And the professional businesswoman turns to writing in hopes of earning credibility in her field. These people are niche writers.

Someone who is passionate about writing, whether they yearn to earn a living in this profession or not, most likely will write about anything within the realm of their interest and understanding. But it's still useful to establish some boundaries. This is where niche writing comes in.

I think it's important to define your writing style. It used to be that when someone asked me what I write, I suddenly felt overwhelmed. My mind would dart from subject to subject as I attempted to come up with a definitive response. I realized that I needed a "nutshell" reply because that's what people expect.

I can say that I write nonfiction. But that's pretty broad. When I thought more about it, however, I realized that my articles and books fall into a handful of categories: family/parenting, lifestyle, the soft side of business, health, animals, spirituality and writing. I write mainly profile and reporting pieces, essays and how to books and articles.

I find it's best, when talking about my work, to just mention my most current book project or talk about a few of my most recent articles.

might say, for example, "I just finished a book on youth mentoring and I'm working on an article about women who work with animals for a local women's magazine." A statement like that usually represents my work appropriately and satisfies the curiosity of anyone who asks. It's also a good conversation starter.

Do you have a specialty? Are you seeking a niche market? Maybe you teach dance or music and that's what you want to write about. Other niche writing might include wildlife, wilderness activities, water sports, building and renovation, photography, business, finance, crafts, gay and lesbian, politics or religion/spirituality, for example.

So how does one find appropriate publications for a niche interest? Here's what I suggest:

- Study *Writer's Market, Literary Market Place* and other sources of magazine editors and book publishers.
- Subscribe to writer's magazines and newsletters.
- Become familiar with online sites for freelance writers.
- Research associations, organizations and clubs representing your niche. Some of them publish magazines.
- Do a Google or AltaVista search to locate other publications in your field or area of interest.
- Contact newspapers throughout the U.S. that might use articles on your topic. Start by visiting www.newspapers.com. (Find more listings in Chapter Twelve.)

Don't overlook overlapping opportunities. In other words, if your expertise is in finance, search out finance and money magazines as well as the economics pages in newspapers, of course. But also consider placing financial pieces in other publications. Finances relate to all lifestyles. How about an article on creating your nest egg after a divorce for a women's magazine, ten money saving tips for retirees geared toward a senior publication, how to build a bank account for a college magazine or a piece on spirituality and money for a religious periodical?

If wildlife is your thing, consider offering a children's magazine editor a series of articles designed to teach children respect for wilderness critters and creatures. Various rural and regional magazine editors may welcome articles related to local wildlife. And there are a lot of magazines that might run articles featuring wildlife as it relates to traveling in certain areas.

I once knew a builder who liked to write about home renovation and building projects. His articles appeared in house and home magazines as well as men's, women's and children's publications and regional, craft, woodworking and retirement magazines. He could also approach specialty mags such as those dedicated to birding (designs for building birdhouses), gardening (how to construct a rose arbor, patio bench or split rail fence) and sports (how to build a portable backstop for practicing soccer or batting in a small area).

Most likely you have had a lot of experience in your area of interest. In order to land a writing job, flaunt your expertise. List your credentials and, if applicable, send photos of your work. If you're not an expert but you're knowledgeable and would like to establish yourself as an expert, start adding to your portfolio. Join or establish a related organization, go back to school, teach workshops, put out a newsletter, speak on the topic and/or write a book or pamphlet on the subject.

Here's another idea: create a new product or theory associated with your topic. If you'd like to write on gardening, come up with a new garden tool, a different way of growing summer vegetables or develop a kit for making fresh flower wreaths, for example. Perhaps your interest revolves around the culinary arts. To get noticed, you might create a series of one-dish meal recipes for busy families or select an ethnic theme to gain prominence in your field.

Countless people today are combining their expertise or experience with their passion for writing. With a little planning and forethought, you, too, can discover your writing niche.

# Local History
## A Lucrative Niche Market

Many new writers pen their memoirs as an initial project and others write about their harrowing experiences, overcoming a challenge or their views on a particular issue. Family history is another popular topic for the novice writer. Rather than simply logging genealogical data, write the story of your ancestors. Or go a step further and write the history of your community.

My second major writing project and the largest and most profitable to date, was a comprehensive history of my hometown. The first edition of *The Ojai Valley, An Illustrated History* (Matilija Press, 1983) took me five years to complete. After another intense year of research, I published the revised edition in 1999. This 358-page volume has sold steadily for over twenty years and will probably continue selling for as long as it's available. Not only is it popular with newcomers to our valley and descendants of early pioneers, but also numerous tourists buy it and carry it back to their own hometowns.

If you're a history buff or if you'd like to document the story of your community, here's my step-by-step guide to writing your local history:

**Determine the need.** Does your community have an interesting history? Has anyone ever captured it on paper? In my preliminary research, I discovered that there had been a lot written about the Ojai Valley over the years, but the material had never been collected and presented under one cover. There were small pamphlets that only touched on local history, numerous magazine and newspaper articles archived away and a multitude of individual stories as yet untold.

Part of determining the need for a written history of your town is figuring out who will read it. Talk to the librarian, the director of the chamber of commerce, the city manager, teachers, docents at the museum and local merchants about whether they see a need for a written history of your area. Ask how they envision a book like this being used. This will help determine your slant and focus. Will it be a small book with just the basic history, a profile of the people who settled and developed the community, a chronicle of historic events, an account of historic places or all of the above?

**Who will publish your book?** Before I started this monumental project, I went in search of a publisher. The local newspaper publisher said he would produce it. He backed out, however, when I held fast to my convictions to create this book for the community. He was looking at this as a touristy item.

I wrote the book not knowing how I would get it published. Ultimately, I decided to self-publish and this was before self-publishing was fashionable, convenient and relatively inexpensive. Today, you can design and prepare a book yourself and have copies printed as you need them through a print-on-demand company. Consider selling ads to display in your book to help with publishing expenses.

If you prefer that someone else publish your book, submit a proposal to the daily newspaper publisher, the area or state historical society, a local philanthropist or a regional publisher. (Read how to write a book proposal on page 62.)

**Research the history.** As mentioned above, I spent five years researching the history of the Ojai Valley. I spent months at the library pouring over early newspapers. I also researched library and museum records and collections throughout several counties. And I interviewed historians, old-timers, descendents of pioneers and people involved in annual events and historic places. I interviewed the woman who started the Biblical Gardens at the Presbyterian Church, for example, the son of an early forest ranger, the original curator for the local museum, the family of the first stable owner in town, the woman who started the community orchestra, and so forth.

Through diligent exploration, I also located people and organizations who had old letters, scrapbooks, record books and other memorabilia. A local water district had a scrapbook depicting the building of our most significant dam, for example. A famous theosophical organization here in the community shared their 60-year-old photo album with me. One pioneer descendant had a box full of old letters.

Talk about your project everywhere you go and you will be given more leads than you can follow. While some of them will be dead ends, many will provide you with incredible information.

During the research phase, ask your local newspaper to do an article about your project and publicly invite people to contact you with their stories.

**Organize the information.** The material for a project like this can become overwhelming. It's crucial to your sanity that you figure out a way to organize it. Here's my method. While in the research phase, I carried a steno pad (lined tablet) everywhere I went. When researching newspapers, for example, I'd note a variety of information, dates, names and events. At home, I'd cut up the pages, organize the material according to subject and file each topic appropriately. I labeled file folders with titles such as: "churches," "cemeteries," "early pioneers," "the business district," "schools," "events" and so forth.

**Collect old photographs.** If you want to illustrate your book, gather photos as you do research and conduct interviews. Ask about old photos everywhere you go. Gathering pictures today is as easy as scanning the photo and saving it on a CD.

**Define your chapters**. When you've come to the end of the research process, it's time to start building your book. First, establish a logical chapter sequence. Will you organize your book chronologically or by popular attractions, events and sites? Maybe you'll want to introduce early settlers and tell the history through their stories.

Next, organize the file folders according to your chapter sequence.

**Start writing.** The first thing you should write is an outline. Take the material from the file folder representing chapter one, organize it in appropriate order and proceed to write an outline. Repeat this process for each chapter. Most likely, you'll find information and data suited to chapter two in the chapter eight file. That's okay. This is your opportunity to make adjustments and corrections. In fact, your book may take on many forms before it's organized the way you want it.

Start writing from your outline. I prefer to start at the beginning, but if your chapters are pretty cut and dried, you could start with the most important chapter and work from there. Some people feel more confident writing the easiest chapters first.

**Verify the facts.** You'll find that some facts are practically etched in stone, while others seem to change before your very eyes. Follow the trail of elusive facts as closely as possible. If you still can't substantiate something, either forget it or, if it's an interesting story, include it with qualifiers, such as, "According to folklore," or "I'm told by several old timers that…" or "Old Jake remembers it this way…"

**Market your book.** Start planning your marketing strategy even before writing your book. For example, fill your book with names. Write about early pioneers, list the folks you interviewed and/or who loaned you photographs, quote the locals you talked to and by all means note the agencies and organizations that worked with you on this project. People love to see their name in print. Everyone you've listed will surely buy at least one book and many of them will buy several copies.

Create and maintain a mailing list of these folks and everyone else you meet who expresses even a remote interest in your book project. Add your Christmas card list, class reunion list, member list for your organizations and so forth. Once the book is published, send flyers or a personal letter to everyone on your mailing list.

Notify bookstore owners, the buyer for the museum gift shop and others as to when your book will be available so they can alert their customers.

Suggest your book as a premium item for local businesses. A bank might give away a book to each new customer, for example. Realtors might want to use your book as a gift for their clients. Consider offering them a bulk rate.

As soon as your book is published, send press releases to local newspapers and radio and TV stations. Follow up with a call suggesting an interview.

Send a flyer to the school district, library system and city hall. My Ojai history book is in every local school library and there are numerous copies in the county library system. Also, each Ojai City Council member has a copy of my book in his or her drawer in council chambers.

You don't have to be a historian in order to write a book on history. All it takes is diligence and persistence, good research and interview skills, an interest in your community and a love of writing.

# Writing Close to Home

Are you so busy searching for a great story in exotic places that you don't notice what's going on right under your nose? You may be surprised at the number of good article and book ideas to be discovered in your own hometown. All you need is a keen eye and an inquisitive mind.

Most of my published books stemmed from local events or contacts. Approximately one-third of my articles published in 2002 (representing a quarter of my income) were generated locally.

Here are some tips for using your friendly neighborhood resources and experts to produce articles and books you can sell Internationally.

1: **View your community with a journalistic eye.** Notice what's going on around you, attend events, visit new businesses and shop locally. Stop by the Humane Society's grand reopening celebration. Tour nearby historic places. Join a local group for a nature hike next Sunday morning. The article ideas should abound.

I'm not a member of the local Chamber of Commerce but, because of some of my other affiliations, I'm sometimes invited to attend their monthly meetings. At a recent Chamber Mixer, I met a woman who had just developed her own line of skin care products for cancer patients. Of course, I set an appointment for an interview with her.

A few weeks ago, I delivered a supply of my local history books to a quilt shop in town. Before leaving, I looked around the store and found a most unique item for sale there. I interviewed the shop owner, took photos of the products, wrote a query letter and landed an assignment with *The Quilter Magazine* within a few days.

2: **Become a tourist in your hometown**. Typically, we travel the same well-worn pathways in our communities, thus we miss out on some of the things tourists enjoy. I suggest occasionally assuming a tourists role. You may be surprised at what you'll find. A recent visit to a local raptor rehabilitation center culminated in an article for *ASPCA Animal Watch*. I've written several articles featuring Bart's Books, a unique outdoor bookstore in Ojai.

3: **Rely on local experts**. Whether I'm writing for a local publication or a national magazine, I often solicit the help of local experts. Sometimes this leads to a full-blown article like the one I did for Silicon2.0 featuring the founder of the highly successful business, Lynda.com. A friend of mine who's a family counselor and involved in helping stepfamilies blend more harmoniously, was an expert for my piece on getting along in a stepfamily. The same woman lost her husband unexpectedly and she participated in a story I wrote for *The Family* on how to help a child through the grieving process. When *PetAge* assigned an article on stress relief products for pets, I interviewed the proprietor of a local natural pet supply store. I also tapped into a few local couples who run businesses together for a piece published in *Business Start-Ups Magazine*. And area Toastmaster members have participated often in my articles for *The Toastmaster Magazine*.

4: **Read the newspaper** to discover what's going on. I'm currently pitching a story about the Volunteer Corps being used at one of this nation's 12 water monuments, the local Channel Islands Sanctuary. I read about this pilot program in the newspaper.

5: **Get involved**. Join in and reap big writing benefits. My involvement with the Ojai Valley Youth Foundation has resulted in one published book and another that I just completed for a publisher. Your volunteer work at the museum might certainly prompt articles for *National Preservationists Magazine*. Maybe you play a ukulele or harmonica in a community orchestra. You might write about the benefits of a community orchestra or how to organize a band. Additional story ideas might emerge from your experiences walking dogs at the local animal shelter, your participation in community theater or the benefit ball you helped organize.

6: **Network with your ears wide open**. Always be on the lookout for potential stories. Years ago, I heard about an Ojai woman who created beautiful cloth dolls with batik faces. I interviewed her and sold her story to a craft magazine. Another local woman had an unusual way of drying flowers. The same magazine was interested in her technique. At a local Little League game, I met a man who was a storyteller. I sold several articles based on my extensive interview with him. Pay attention when your neighbor tells you about the teen down the street who runs his own company, a couple who grow herbs for local gourmet restaurants or the man who has recipes for cactus apples. These stories could earn you a paycheck.

7: **Look for local stories that have national appeal**. While some local stories have a better chance of success in local regional publications, others might make it into a national or international magazine. There is a group of dogs here in Ojai, for example, that have participated in the search and rescue efforts after the Oklahoma City bombing and in New York after 9/11. Of course, their story has made news all over the world. Ojai is the world center for Krotona Institute, Meditation Mount and other such institutions. Stories about these organizations have been reported internationally.

Is your community home to the winningest pee wee soccer team in the state? Do you have the highest percentage of health conscious teens? Is there something noteworthy about this year's high school graduating class? Have city officials found a way to deter incidents of tagging? Follow the story. It may lead you to riches—or at least a byline in a national magazine.

As you can see by my examples, the article possibilities lurking in your hometown are endless. Stop taking your community for granted. Start looking for the story and you will find it.

# Write for the Regionals

If you're like most freelance writers, you submit articles to national magazines and you query the editors of special interest journals, but you don't pursue regional publications. Do you have any idea what you're missing by not exploring the regional market?

*Writer's Market* has nearly 50 pages of regional magazines or about 150 listings. Altogether, this collection of regional magazines publish approximately 5,000 articles per year and they pay anywhere from $25 to $5,000 per article with the average in the $300-$500 range. And there are always new regional magazines cropping up. We've featured over thirty new ones in the monthly SPAWN Market Update during the past fifteen months. (The Market Update appears in the Member Area of the SPAWN Web site at www.spawn.org).

Of course, a good place to start is locally. Discover your own community and state publications. Interview the girl who made the junior varsity football team at your local high school for a city youth magazine. Write about the volunteers behind your community's entry in a major New Year's Day parade for a county publication. Or suggest a piece featuring the haunted houses in your city for a monthly throw away paper.

I once wrote an article for a local technology magazine featuring county teen entrepreneurs who had established businesses in the technology field. They also published my two-part story featuring local women who are making their mark in technology. I mentioned earlier that I sold an article about a unique item I found at a local quilt shop to a quilting magazine. I also wrote a piece for a local food publication because the item was related to food. When the quilt shop owner realized that she wasn't moving certain shades of fabric, she began packaging it to resemble food. It's an interesting story. Now this fabric, in the form of cinnamon rolls, green salads and orange drinks is selling like hotcakes.

**Write about the places you've visited**. Tourists often have a different perspective than those people who live in a community. As a visitor, you notice the things residents only take for granted. The last time I visited my brother and his family in Winchester, Idaho, I came home and queried *Northwest Travel* about a piece on this small, out of the way lakeside town. The article is scheduled to run this winter.

Maybe while touring the west coast last summer, a particular site or place of business piqued your interest. With a little research and a fresh angle, you might be able to sell *Oregon Coast, Seattle Weekly* or *San Francisco Magazine* on your idea. Do you have relatives in Chicago? Pay for a trip to visit them by writing articles for some of the many regional magazines published in Illinois.

**Share your childhood memories**. Whether you grew up in the state where you live or in another community, you have a unique perspective about life during that era. Some regional magazines love to publish nostalgia pieces. *Back Home in Kentucky*, is one. Others include: *Louisville Magazine, Baltimore Magazine, Cape Cod Life, Traverse (*Northern Michigan's Magazine*), New Jersey Living* and *Charlotte Magazine*.

Share stories of your first encounter with a bear while camping in an obscure campground in that state. Write about the first parade to roll down the main street of your hometown. Or describe the teen hangout that was once on the site of what has become a controversial construction project.

**Write from afar**. You don't have to live in or even visit a city or a state in order to write for their regional magazines. Information is so accessible now that you can research nearly any aspect of the place from your home. And you can do necessary interviews by email or phone.

For example, I've been locating library cats throughout the U.S. and querying appropriate magazines about articles featuring those library cats in their region. I contacted *New Hampshire Magazine* about library cats in the New Hampshire area, for example, *Southern Living* about a piece on library and shop cats in the southern states and *Ohio Magazine,* hoping they would publish my article on Ohio library cats.

You might query the editors of *Texas Highways* regarding an article featuring a little known historical aspect of Texas—an early hotel, an interesting figure or a long forgotten shoot-out, for example. Are you aware of a little known but fascinating sports figure from New Jersey? Contact Christopher Hann at the *New Jersey Monthly* with your story and earn yourself up to $2000.

While most editors want only local material for their regional publications, others are open to more general topics. I sold an article on how to present a luau to *North Georgia Journal*. *Northwest Family, L. A. Parent, Seattle's Child, South Florida Parent* and *Central CA Parent* each published some of my general child-rearing articles. I even sold my article on how to successfully use small talk in business to *Florida Realtors*.

This year, make a commitment to step outside your comfort zone and break into the wide-open field of regional magazines. Set a goal. You might commit to sending five or ten queries to regional magazines each week. Come up with at least one new idea for a regional magazine each month. This might mean traveling, keeping a finger on the pulse of other areas through friends and acquaintances, reading obscure history books, keying in on the daily news and/or reading travel magazines.

Add regional magazines to your repertoire and you'll automatically increase your annual income.

# Write About Where You've Been

In good times and bad, one topic that never seems to lose its appeal or go out of style is travel. There are numerous travel publications and countless other magazines, ezines, Web sites and newspapers that print destination pieces. These publications and sites have two main types of readers: those who are seriously planning a trip and those who are only dreaming of going somewhere. In either case, they want to read interesting, informative articles about faraway places.

Do you like to travel? Can you write accurate, detailed accounts of potential vacation spots and little-known places? Then you might consider joining those dedicated writers who devote their lives to travel writing.

Who buys travel pieces? Most medium and large newspapers publish a travel section. Regional magazines are generally interested in travel articles related to their area. Many specialty magazines use an occasional travel piece: *Grace Ormonde Wedding Style, Friendly Exchange, Grit* and *The Atlantic Monthly*, for example. Travel writers can also score with in-flight, general travel and trade travel magazines.

Often, when someone decides to be a travel writer, that's all they do and for good reason. They spend a lot of their time traveling. Once established, they get complimentary stays at bed and breakfast inns, at resorts, on cruise ships and so forth. When they aren't relaxing with a gourmet meal or touring a little-known stretch of beach, they're reliving these experiences by writing about them. This may sound like your ideal lifestyle. But not every writer is cut out for it.

**Travel writing is about paying attention to detail**. Everyone who visits Seattle sees the space needle. But a good travel writer will also notice the charming pet shop just outside of town that hosts an animal psychic every week or the saltwater taffy vender who will snap a picture of you pulling taffy.

**Travel writing means good observation skills**. Train your eye to see beyond the obvious. Don't go to Hawaii with the idea of walking the well-worn paths from a tourist's point of view. Live with the people, talk to them, join in on their events. Tell the stories of their land through their words and emotions.

**A travel writer should have an affinity with history**. You can add greatly to a destination story by weaving local history into it. A little Internet research before you leave, and time spent in the museum there and talking to residents might add flavors not available from just your point of view.

**A travel writer must be open to adventure**. Take the footpath instead of the tram to the top of the mountain. Fish with natives off the rocks at Neah Bay. Go behind the scenes at the jai alai arena.

**A travel writer should be a skilled photographer.** Sure you can illustrate your magnificent article by using stock photos, but will they portray the story as it unraveled for you? (Read more about photography for writers on page 111.)

**Become a tourist in your own hometown**. To start a career as a travel writer, write about your own city or an interesting town nearby. Cover a local strawberry festival or a unique book fair for the travel section of a large newspaper or a travel magazine.

Locate interesting places in your county and write about them—a house made out of bottles that has been turned into a museum, a turn of the century olive mill that has been restored, a small airport where they offer panoramic tours of the skyline or a unique artists' retreat.

If you have the vacation story of the century, you might have a chance with some of the major travel magazines such as *National Geographic Traveler* or *Travel and Leisure*. But most travel writers start by selling good features to smaller publications. A reliable travel writer who makes a good impression will usually be rewarded with additional assignments.

For camaraderie, inspiration and solid leads consider joining a travel writers' organization such as: Society of American Travel Writers (www.satw.org); International Food, Wine and Travel Writers Association (www.ifwtwa.org)

or North American Travel Journalists Association (www.natja.org). Check out the following sites for information about travel magazines: Travelwriters.com lists over 600 travel publications and 200 newspapers with travel sections (www.travelwriters.com). Also check out Wooden Horse Publications at www.woodenhorsepubs.com and Writer's Market.com at www.writersmarket.com.

Learn the ins and outs of travel writing by signing up for an online class at: www.WritingSchool.com, www.WritingClasses.com or www.WritersCollege.com

Follow the guidelines outlined here and soon your motto will be, "Have pen will travel."

## Chapter Four

..........................
### Get Published Now

♦ Organize Your Nonfiction Book in 10 Easy Steps

♦ Make Your Book More Salable

♦ The Book Proposal: Put Your Best Foot Forward

♦ How to Get the Publisher to Say "Yes"

♦ Develop a Working Relationship With Your Publisher

# Organize Your Nonfiction Book
# In 10 Easy Steps

There are probably more people in the world who *don't* write th
book that's rattling around inside them than who do. Why? They simp
don't know how to begin.

Are you overwhelmed by the idea of putting your story down on pape
Here's a guide to help you actually write that book:

**Come up with a good idea**. Make the topic of your book somethir
that you know and find extremely interesting. You should have a passic
for your subject because it's going to be a part of your life not ju
during the time that it takes you to write it, but for as long as you ha
books to sell.

I recently asked a first-time author how his book was doing. H
grimaced and said, "I'm afraid I'm kind of burned out on that book
After three years spent writing and rewriting his book and anothe
year trying to market it, he had lost interest. And part of the reasc
was that he chose a subject based only on what he thought would se
and not something that also excited him.

**Study the market for a book like yours.** Visit bookstores, examir
the listings in reference books such as *Writer's Market* and *Literar
Market Place* and look at what's available on the Internet an
Amazon.com. Is the market saturated with books on this subject?
so, what can you offer that's different? If not, is this something tha
readers really want? Contact a couple of publishers to see if your ide
is viable in today's market. Talk to experts in this field and potentia
readers. Would they welcome a book like the one you have planned

**Identify your audience**. Who are you writing for? Avoid focusing s
narrowly that you eliminate readers and so widely that the book can'
be pigeonholed. When I decided to write a book on book marketing
for example, I could have limited it to marketing just true crime book
or just poetry books and my audience would have diminishe

considerably. If, on the other hand, I chose to write about marketing in general without focusing on a specific commodity, I've lost touch with my audience and marketing the book becomes extremely complicated.

**Gather material and contact experts**. The research process will serve two purposes: You'll discover whether you can locate enough information to justify an entire book and you'll have a jumpstart on compiling the book.

**Get organized**. Store research material and contact information in file folders according to topic or possible chapters. I use cardboard file boxes to hold the material I'm gathering for a book project. I just completed a book on youth mentoring, for example. I filed the material as I collected it in file folders labeled: introduction, one-on-one-mentoring, mentor-mentee activities, neighborhood mentoring, school-based mentor programs, resource list and so forth. When it came time to write the book, my chapters practically fell into place.

**Discipline yourself to write the book**. Procrastination has halted or delayed many a great book from being produced. If you have a life, it isn't easy to add an activity as intense and time-consuming as writing a book. If this is your dream, however, be prepared to make some sacrifices. (Refer to the chapter on page 13 for more help in this area.)

**Develop a book proposal**. This is a big job, but it's not wasted motion. A book proposal will reveal whether or not you actually have a book. Can you describe your book adequately in one or two paragraphs? Can you create a detailed chapter outline? Have you thought about how this book will be marketed? What is the scope of competition for this book? Whether you plan to self-publish or locate a traditional publisher, the process of writing a book proposal should be your first step in writing the book. For help in writing a book proposal refer to *The Author's Toolkit* by Mary Embree (Allworth Press, 2003) or *Write the Perfect Book Proposal* by Herman and Adams (John Wiley and Sons, Inc., 1993). Read more about book proposals on page 62.

**Write the book**. By now you've established a writing routine and you have an outline and sample chapters. While a book always needs beginning, middle and end, you don't necessarily have to start writing the beginning. Start wherever it's comfortable and just let your words flow. Go back and make corrections and adjustments later. And don't be concerned if it takes you a few hours and several pages before you've written something you actually like. Keep writing and the magic will happen.

**Edit, edit, edit** and then hire someone to edit some more. Even professional, well-read authors need fresh eyes to view their work before it's ready for the public.

**Create a marketing plan**. Before starting the book, you should be thinking about marketing it. This is true whether you decide to self-publish or locate a traditional publisher. In my book, *Over 75 Good Ideas for Promoting Your Book* (Matilija Press, 2000), I offer criteria for making your book a salable item. That's number one in establishing your marketing plan. (Read more about making your book salable on page 60.)

Secondly, know what you're getting into. Marketing a book is intense work that demands several years of your time. Review my book and others specific to book marketing before even thinking about writing a book of your own.

Most new authors expect to see their wonderful book jumping off of the shelves in mega-bookstores nationwide. The truth is that bookstores aren't necessarily the best place to sell your book. Marketing a book these days takes study and creativity. For example, statistics indicate that there are more books for sale at specialty shops of various kinds than in bookstores. (Reference the articles in Chapter Six for more about book marketing.)

**Decide whether to self publish or find a traditional publisher**. Be informed before making this decision. Read Dan Poynter's *Self Publishing Manual* (Para Publishing). Talk to other authors. Join SPAWN and join in on the online forum where members can exchange information and ideas about publishing options with other members. Many authors today have just a few copies of their books printed by a print-on-demand (POD) company to see how well they are accepted before going out on a limb and ordering thousands of copies they can't sell.

Sometimes it's worthwhile to self-publish your book, work hard to promote it and, after it has proven it's value, approach a traditional publisher. Mary Embree self-published *The Author's Toolkit*. A review in *Library Journal* resulted in a great many sales. So when she approached Allworth Press with the book, they were immediately interested. I self-published my book on presenting a Hawaiian luau on the mainland. My intense marketing plan paid off. Book sales impressed a Hawaiian publisher and they issued me a contract.

As you can see, there's more to becoming a published author than just writing your story. Follow these steps and you, too, will live your dream.

# Make Your Book More Salable
(Excerpted from *Over 75 Good Ideas for Promoting Your Book*)

Tending to business issues such as getting an ISBN and a bar code are important steps to making your self-published book salable. (Reference the article on page 81 for additional information.) There's more that you can do, however, to ensure sales even before putting pen to paper or fingers to keyboard. Yes, even prior to writing that book, you need to be thinking about how you're going to sell it. Here are four easy steps to making your book more marketable:

1. **Research books on your topic**. How many are there? How are they selling? Can you define a market for your book? An honest and thorough study might alter the scope and focus of your book.

Maybe you planned to write the history of scooters and skateboards in America. Through research, however, you discover a lack of books and, seemingly, a greater need for a book on building custom scooters and skateboards.

A comparative study for a book about the life of a feral cat might prompt you to develop a guide to getting involved with feral cat colonies in your community, instead.

Find out about published books on your topic by doing a search on www.amazon.com. Explore books shelved at a nearby mega bookstore. Look up books on your topic in *Books in Print* and *Forthcoming Books in Print* at your local library or on the Internet.

You can actually test the market like Barbara Saltzman did. Shortly before he died, Barbara's son, David, wrote a children's book called. *The Jester Has Lost His Jingle*. Wanting to carry on his legacy, but needing feedback before launching the project, Barbara test-marketed the book. She invited mothers to read it to their children and asked the moms to observe the response. Pleased with the children's reaction to the book, Barbara and her husband became very successful publishers.

2. **Involve a lot of people in your book and build numerous promotional angles into it.** When I wrote *The Ojai Valley, An Illustrated History*, I included a list of all the people I interviewed for this book. I listed the individuals, organizations and companies that loaned me photographs and material. I quoted people in the text where appropriate. Before I even started marketing the book, I knew of about 150 people who would probably buy at least one copy of it. Everyone likes to see his or her name in print.

3. **Write a book that will appeal to a wide range of people.** You might figure out a way to tie the theme of your book or a character in your book to a national organization that encompasses a particular group of people such as, those with disabilities, volunteers, educators, healthcare workers and so forth.

I have a book in the works about the joy of solitude. To attract more readers, I'm including chapters for widows and widowers, those experiencing empty nest syndrome, divorced men and women, college students, single parents, people who have relocated to a new community and are lonely, retirees, individuals who feel alone in a relationship, people who are caring for an ailing relative alone and grandparents raising grandchildren alone. Obviously this book will draw thousands more readers than if it was directed strictly to those who are divorced, for example. And my marketing opportunities are far more expansive.

4. **Promote your book while you're writing it.** Start getting people excited about your book by talking it up everywhere you go. And, while you're at it, compile an extensive mailing list. I know, you prefer seeing your book exhibited at Barnes and Noble in the middle aisle. We all do. But don't get so caught up in your lofty dreams that you neglect the obvious sales—those to friends and acquaintances.

It's tricky trying to second-guess the public. Even large publishing company executives have trouble predicting the market. We can assess the potential market to the best of our abilities, however, and we should before ever going to the trouble to produce a book.

# The Book Proposal
## Put Your Best Foot Forward

The first time I heard the term *book proposal*, I quickly changed the subject. I didn't even want to know what it entailed because I wasn't going to write one. I had a completed manuscript and a cover letter. What more could a publisher want?

Since that day many years ago, I have written over a dozen book proposals. I've learned that a well-designed book proposal is an excellent marketing tool. It gives a publisher the information he/she needs in order to evaluate your project. But it also makes your life easier because you can use it as a guide to writing your book.

Probably the best thing about writing a book proposal is that during the process, you'll find out if you truly have a book at all. As Mary Embree points out in her book, *The Author's Toolkit* (Allworth Press, 2003), there are at least six major things you can learn about your project as you go through the steps of developing a book proposal. Here is her list in condensed form.

You will learn:
- how to focus on your subject
- how to describe your book to others
- how to organize your material
- whether you have a salable idea
- how to sell the book yourself
- what your competition is.

I suggest writing the book proposal even *before* sending query letters to potential publishers. You will be prepared, should the publisher ask to see your proposal. You're ready to write the book because it's already outlined. And if you decide to self-publish, you've got a jumpstart on marketing it.

Here, we're focusing on the nonfiction book proposal. While publishers and agents sometimes request proposals for novels, they are not quite the same. According to Embree, a fiction proposal doesn't have as many parts. She says, "The proposal for a novel might have only the title page, a synopsis and an author bio."

Here's what goes into a nonfiction book proposal:

**Cover Letter**. Write a formal letter on your letterhead that identifies your package as a book proposal. Post your title here. List the parts you've included (Synopsis, Promotional Ideas, About the Author and so forth). And give a projected completion or delivery date for the manuscript. If the book is finished, say so.

**Title Page**. On this page, center your title using an attractive (but readable) font in 14-point type or larger. The authors' names go under the title in smaller letters. "Your title should be provocative and succinct," says Embree. "Short titles are usually preferred by publishers and they are easier for potential readers to remember." But she suggests, "You can add a subtitle if you think that your short title doesn't tell enough about the book."

Some authors write a brief description of their book on the title page. If your title and subtitle adequately describe your book, however, this is probably not necessary. Avoid clutter. Strive for clarity and simplicity in your presentation.

I also include my projected word count at the bottom of the title page. How do you determine your word count? I base this on each individual publisher's requirements. Before sending a query letter, request the publisher's Guidelines for Writers. Your proposed word count should be within their standards. And by the time you complete your book proposal, you should have a fairly clear idea as to how many words you can actually deliver.

**Synopsis or Overview**. The synopsis is the meat of your book proposal. This is where you describe your story or the theme and purpose of your book. If you can't write a one or two-page synopsis, you'd better rethink your idea. According to Embree, "The synopsis should have a beginning, middle and end, just as your book does. Tell how your book opens, what it is about and how it ends. You may want to give some of the highlights, specific events, dialogue or unknown facts."

How important is the synopsis or overview? According to Jeff Herman and Deborah Adams, authors of *Write the Perfect Book Proposal*, "The overview can open—or close—the door for you." And they challenge authors to consider what they would say if they had five minutes face-to-face with a publisher. Put that kind of energy, effort and perfection into your synopsis.

**Enhancements.** As far as I know, this page is of my own creation. This is where I list the experts I'll be working with on this project and their affiliations. For my Creative Grandparenting book, for example, I listed about a dozen individuals and grandparents' agencies that I had already contacted. In my Fatherhood and Fathering book proposal, I listed nearly thirty. And I mentioned here that I planned to provide a photograph of a father and child for the beginning of each chapter.

If you plan illustrations for your book or have an idea for a specific design, you might provide samples here for the publisher.

Note: Never send original artwork with your proposal.

**Promotional Ideas**. Today, publishers need to know that the author is willing to help promote his or her book. If you're affiliated with a large organization related to your book topic, say so. If you are a skilled public speaker, mention that. I know a cookbook author who landed a publisher because of a commitment from a national kitchen store to carry her book.

You should have plenty of ideas about who will buy this book and how it should be marketed. Share these ideas with potential publishers.

**Market Analysis**. For this section, you will research books similar to yours and explain how yours will differ. What makes your book stand out from the rest?

**About the Author**. Here, you will offer your bio. Include your writing experience and education as well as your involvement and/or expertise related to your proposed book topic. I introduce myself as a working writer with 30 years experience writing for publication. I list some of the magazines I've written for—especially those relating to my topic. I also list my published books. And I include a list of books in the works. Sometimes a publisher will ask to see something from this list.

Give the publisher every reason to be interested in you and to trust you as the author of this book. A good track record can be an impressive foot-in-the-door.

**Chapter Outline**. Here's where you really find out if you have a book. List each chapter by title and briefly describe the proposed content. If you can't outline 8 or 10 chapters, you probably don't have a book. Either think smaller—an article or pamphlet, or do more research.

**Sample Chapters.** Often, but not always, the proposal includes sample chapters. Some publishers will specify that they want to see anywhere from one to three sample chapters. Generally, you want to send Chapter One and the chapter that you feel is most powerful or most important.

A book proposal is a necessity in today's publishing climate. So you might as well bite the bullet and decide to write one for your manuscript. Once you've broken through the mystery of your first book proposal, you'll be surprised at how vital the proposal is to your project and how effortlessly future book proposals will go together.

# How to Get the Publisher to Say "Yes"

You've worked hard on your perfect manuscript. You're ready to send it to a publisher. What can you do to ensure a positive response? Following are eight techniques that have worked for other authors.

1: **Have the manuscript edited *before* submitting it**. Never present a manuscript that reflects anything less than your best effort. That means submitting a completely edited manuscript. I know one author who got a second chance. He presented his manuscript to an agent only to be told, "You get this professionally edited and I'll take another look at it." He hired an editor, resubmitted it and, not only did the agent decide to represent this author, she found a publisher for his book within a matter of months.

2: **Follow submission guidelines**. While most publishers' guidelines are similar, some vary. It's important to be familiar with the submission guidelines for each publisher you contact and to follow them. If the publisher outlines specific items that he wants in the book proposal, revise your generic proposal to reflect his wishes. He may want your proposal to include three sample chapters. Write those chapters. If it will take a little time, tell the publisher when he can expect receipt of the proposal. I recommend completing the assignment within three-six weeks.

3: **Contact the right person.** It happened to me again last week. I addressed my query to the woman I thought was the most current contact person for a particular publishing company only to have my letter returned. Someone wrote on the package, "This editor is no longer with this publishing house." Obviously, I didn't care which editor read my letter. I just wanted it read. Why didn't they hand it over to the current editor? Maybe it's the busy editor's way of saying, "If you can't do your homework and address your letter correctly, we aren't even going to look at it." This gross oversight on my part cost me time and embarrassment. And it wouldn't have occurred had I followed my own advice and called the publishing offices to inquire as to the appropriate contact person.

3: **Meet deadlines**. Publishers' deadlines are not always reasonable. I was asked last year to write a 50,000-word book in three months. Of course, the publisher had held my proposal package for almost two years before issuing me a contract. I told them that I was willing to meet their deadline but, because I would have to stop my other work and wouldn't be earning an income, I needed a large advance. Instead, they extended my deadline and offered a lesser amount. I completed the manuscript with six-weeks to spare.

4: **Be flexible.** When I interview publishers for the *SPAWN Market Update*, I often ask, "What type of author do you prefer?" And the response is usually, "Authors who are easy to work with." In other words, they want authors who can go with the flow and who are willing to make necessary changes to their project. I met a wannabe author over the weekend who has written a 150,000-word novel or the equivalent of around 450 pages. Every publisher he has approached so far suggests that he cut the size of the book. Some have told him that they don't publish books that large by first-time authors. This gentleman, however, is firmly attached to his story just the way it is. He claims that by shortening it, it's not the story he wants to tell. It is authors like this man who confirm how difficult it is to break into the publishing business. He'll go through life blaming the publishing industry for his failure, when in fact, he has turned his back on his own success.

5: **Tout your promotional abilities**. The publisher wants to know that you have the interest, skills and time to promote your book. Reveal your affiliations with organizations and agencies that could help boost your book sales. List your marketing skills and promotional ideas. Are you a public speaker? Do you have the funds to hire a publicist? Share your future plans. One client of mine got a publisher to say "yes" after she told him that she was about to retire and would devote her time to promoting her book. Don't keep these things a secret. Make them a strong part of your book proposal.

**7: Give the publisher something extra**. Perhaps you're seeking a publisher for your high seas adventure novel. Don't hide the fact that you've won several contests for your short stories on this topic. If the story you're pitching has been highly publicized, send the publisher a couple of the most provocative newspaper articles. One of my clients did a televised interview related to the true crime story he had written. With permission, we sent a videotape of the show to a prospective publisher along with a copy of the letter of invitation to do another segment once the book is published. This turned out to be a contributing factor to the book being accepted.

**8: Brag about your upcoming books and ideas**. Many publishers, when they find a book and an author they like, want to parlay their good fortune. If you plan a sequel or have a similar idea for one or more additional books, be sure to talk it up. If you don't, it would be a wise move to start planning another bestseller. Let's say that you're pitching a book on photography for the beginner. Follow-up topics might include, photography for children, video photography for the beginner and so forth.

Landing a publisher is not always easy, but you can increase your odds by doing all of the right things.

# Develop a Working Relationship
## With Your Publisher

Congratulations! You've landed a publisher. But don't relax, yet. Now, you need to figure out how to work with him or her. Follow this guide and you should enjoy a good working relationship with your publisher for the life of your contract.

1: **Respect the publisher's time and space**. Respond with just the information requested and send just the material required. Do not, for example, inundate the publisher with frequent phone calls. Don't send several video tapes showing you speaking before the local Rotary Club, the correspondence between yourself and your editor for the last several months or the first eight drafts of your manuscript unless he/she asks for it.

2: **Be prompt with proofs and rewrites**. Always ask if there is a deadline. If not, project one for yourself and share it with the publisher. Say, for example, "I can have this to you by the end of the month, is that okay?" Once a deadline is established, do your absolute best to meet it.

3: **Keep yourself in the loop**. You deserve respect, too, and respect for an author means being included in the project. I do not suggest calling the publisher every few days to see what's up. Rather, try to keep an open line of communication with him or her. Ask the publisher to share his/her calendar with regard to your project. If he says that the galleys won't be ready until the end of November, don't call him in September asking if they're ready. If an unreasonable amount of time goes by without word from the publisher, email him or her and request an update. It is usually okay to call a publisher if there is a valid reason. Obviously, some publishers are more organized and better communicators than others. If certain personality types drive you crazy, you might want to reconsider whether or not you can work with this individual before making a commitment to a publishing contract.

**4: Be up front with your publisher**. If you have a deadline, but you'r having trouble reaching someone who is key to your last chapter, fo example, let the publisher know there is a problem and how you plan t rectify it.

**5: Give the publisher your best effort.** A new writer wrote to m recently and asked if she should tell the publisher that she plans to hire a editor after he looks at her manuscript. Of course, I strongly suggeste that she hire that editor *before* sending her work to the publishe Shortchanging your publisher means shortchanging yourself.

**6: Be prepared to hand over control**. Once the contract is signed, th publisher takes control. You'll like some of his/her decisions and other may upset you. Be prepared to see the title of your book changed, fo example, and some of the content.

**7: Expect to rewrite your manuscript**. Just when you thought you book was finished and you're anxious to start the next one, your publishe may ask for a rewrite. Make sure that you have a contract. Sometimes a publisher will ask you to revise your sample chapters before committing to publishing your book. Be careful here. Know in advance how mucl work you are willing to do before the project is accepted. I once go involved with rewriting several chapters of a book for a publisher. In fact he asked me to refocus my entire manuscript. They sent me back to the drawing board three times without so much as a promise of a contract. finally realized that the book they wanted me to write was nothing like the one I wanted to write. And with no contract forthcoming, I decided to withdraw my manuscript.

**8: Request guidance in marketing your book**. While your book i being published, inquire about the company's promotional strategy. Asl for any suggestions they might have for marketing your book and star putting a plan together.

**9: Keep your publisher informed as to your marketing efforts.** Once a month or so, send an email or post a note reporting on your promotiona progress. Say, for example, "I sent press releases to newspapers in the northeast region and review copies to thirty magazines and newsletters. I have two book signings scheduled and last week I spoke before the local branch of the National Association of Business Women and sold twelve books."

10: **Share the good news.** Anytime your book receives a review or an award, an article relating to the book is published or you are quoted, send copies to your publisher. When your publisher sees you putting forth effort toward promoting your book and when he sees the positive results, he'll be more inclined to put more of his energy into your project.

When you have a contract with a publisher, you are responsible for half of the relationship. Hold up your end and your association should go smoothly.

# Chapter Five

....................................

## *Self-Publishing Your Book*

♦ **Self-Publishing Basics**

♦ **How to Assess Your Future in Self-Publishing**

♦ **Publish Your Own Book—a Timeline**

# Self-Publishing Basics

Today's publishing climate offers authors many options. You can submit your work to traditional publishers. If you happen to land one, they will make all of the arrangements for having the book designed and printed, they'll foot the bill and you'll collect royalties.

How much can you expect to get? Generally, anywhere from six to fifteen percent of net—that is, whatever the publisher collects for that book. Most of the books are discounted, so your royalties will be discounted, too. If you get 10 percent royalties on a $10 book and the publisher discounts the book by 40 percent, your cut is 60 cents. And this goes on only for as long as the publisher is willing to promote your book, which might be a mere twelve months.

You can partner with a co-publisher who, with your money, will produce your book, do limited marketing and give you 40 or 50 percent of the profits.

Or you can take control and self-publish your book. Here are the benefits:
- You'll definitely see your book in print.
- You can have a finished product within weeks or months.
- You have the potential to make more money.
- You have all of the control.
- There are tax breaks to owning your own business.
- You are the best possible marketing agent for your project.
- Your book will keep selling for as long as you are willing to market it.

What about the down side?
- Self-publishing and marketing a book is a full-time job.
- Self publishing is costly
- Self-publishing requires a lot of decision-making.
- Promoting a book is 100 times more difficult and time-consuming than writing it.
- Your book will keep selling for as long as you are willing to market it.

If you're still interested in self-publishing, here are some of your options: You can have your book printed through a traditional printer, take it to a print-on-demand (POD) company, print and bind it at home yourself or produce an ebook.

The most cost effective way to produce a quality book is through a traditional printer. But the total output is more because you have to order books in larger quantities. There are often wide differences in quality and price between printers. Ask several printers for price quotes, samples of their work and references. Expect to pay anywhere from $2,000 to $20,000 for 1000 to 5000 copies of your book (depending, of course, on page number, number and type of illustrations, binding style and so forth).

If you want to test the market for your book and/or don't want to store boxes and boxes of books, POD may be the right choice for you. You can have anywhere from five to one hundred books printed at a time, for example. And the turnaround is fast—usually a week to 4 weeks. However, the cost per book is generally higher through a POD company.

An advantage of using a POD company is that you can make changes each time you go to print. I have friends who change the text for their travel guides nearly every time they place an order with their POD company.

Some self-publishers forego the hassle of dealing with outside print companies at all by producing their books in-house. Anyone with a home computer and printer has the capacity to manufacture a book. You can even bind and trim it yourself using a saddle stapler and commercial cutter or plastic comb binding. Some new publishers use this method to test market their books.

For smaller books, booklets and pamphlets, it may be cheaper to let a local business center print, saddle stitch, fold and trim your books. We just had 100 copies of a seventy page book produced at a Kinko's-type store locally for $2.15 per book. This is a dollar more than I paid per book to have 1000 fifty-five page books produced by a traditional printer ten years ago.

By the way, once you've self-published your book and have proven it in the market place, you may be able to interest a publisher in it, if that's your ultimate goal.

A major part of self-publishing is promotion. In fact, some experts say you should set aside as much money for marketing the book as you paid to have it produced. If you're not an aggressive marketer, hire someone who is.

Don't expect to produce a book, do a blast of marketing the first few months and then just sit back and collect money for evermore. A successful self-publisher must have a business head, ongoing enthusiasm for his project and a bent for promotion. Your book can live for as long as you are willing to promote it. Once you stop, however, it will likely die.

Hopefully, you will prepare a book proposal before writing your book and that proposal includes a marketing section. This is where you determine who your audience is and how you will reach them. Be realistic. How will you market your book? Don't assume that Barnes and Noble and Borders will clamor to get copies of your book to stock by the caseload. It's getting more and more difficult for the small publisher to get shelf space in the big bookstores. One way to get their attention is to publicize your book widely and strongly enough that customers start asking for it by name.

Find out where other books on your topic are sold—specialty shops, gift shops, county fairs, the school system... Dan Poynter sold thousands of copies of his parachuting book through skydiving-related shops. My book on presenting a Hawaiian luau did well at Southern barbecue events, barbecue kitchen stores and Hawaiian tourist shops. You might also consider your book as an incentive item for a banking organization or a large company.

Request reviews. Write magazine articles on your topic. Give workshops. Invest in mailing lists involving the demographics of folks who would purchase your book. Send press releases nationwide, if applicable. Draw attention to yourself and your book. If your book is about children who have recovered from cancer, for example, do a fund-raiser for the local cancer association and make sure you get national coverage.

There are numerous things to think about when contemplating self-publishing. Hopefully this article will help you make the decision that's right for you.

# How to Assess Your Future in Self-Publishing

Publishing is not for the faint of heart, the short-sighted or the introvert. It's a commitment that demands courage, risk-taking, planning, energy, creativity and assertiveness.

Before entering into the realm of self-publishing, consider the following:
- Is there an audience for your book?
- Are you willing to take the steps necessary to establish and operate a publishing business?
- Do you have the funds available to pour into your project?
- Do you have room to store boxes and boxes of books?
- Do you have the time and inclination to promote your book?

I know hundreds of authors who have self-published their books. Some have produced a book or a series of books while working a full-time job. Others have one book that they self-published and are marketing until their stock runs out. But most of them have set up a publishing company in order to produce numerous books.

I'm often asked during a workshop or other presentation, which I prefer—going with a traditional publisher or self-publishing? Truth? I like the ease of having a traditional publisher who handles the business end of the project and pays quarterly royalties. I like not being responsible for storing the books. Since I'm still involved in promoting the books even with a publisher, however, I actually prefer self-publishing. I like being in control of the project. When I self-publish, I choose the title and the cover design. I decide what chapters stay and which ones go. But this also means that I have total responsibility for promoting the book.

Certainly, self-publishing is not for everyone. A few months ago, I spoke with someone who yearns to be published, but she doesn't want a paper trail leading to her. She doesn't want to do anything involving public interaction. She probably would not be a good candidate for self-publishing.

Some elderly people may want their memoirs published, but do not relish the hassle of self-publishing—setting up a distribution company, finding a cover designer and printer, promoting the book, taking orders and shipping books, etc.

Someone with a full-time career and who writes a book as a sideline, probably doesn't want to get involved with operating a publishing business.

Anyone on a small income will find it difficult to finance a self-publishing venture.

I often coach authors who want to start their own publishing company and have observed about a fifty percent success ratio. Those who succeed have built a business around their project and they take that business seriously. They have goals and they evaluate their goals regularly. They give their project their full attention. If they lack skills in a particular area, they hire someone to take up the slack.

I know one author, for example, who spent two years operating quite a successful campaign on behalf of her book. The book was reviewed in major newspapers all over the country. She traveled far and wide giving demonstrations and selling books. Through her efforts, an impressive number of books were sold. When she ran out of steam, energy and ideas, she hired a publicist and book sales absolutely soared.

I don't do page layout and design, so I hire someone to perform that task for me. I find shipping and handling large mailings rather mundane and time-consuming. I hire my grandchildren to help with these projects and we do them outside of regular business hours.

You get interesting responses when you tell people that you have a publishing company. Some ask where you keep the printing presses. Others want to discuss having you publish their grandmother's memoirs. Still others call or stop you on the street and say, "I'm thinking about writing a book, how do I go about publishing it?" It is this question multiplied by dozens that prompted me to hang out my shingle. I now charge for consultations.

The discouraging thing is that most people are looking for a shortcut to publishing success. It's after I map out the well-traveled course that the serious authors are culled from the wannabes.

Are you serious about self-publishing? Do you believe in your project enough to put in the effort and time? Or are you looking for a get-rich-quick scheme?

Either way, I suggest that you enter into the world of self-publishing with a viable project, an open mind, creative ideas, lots of energy and a willingness to work hard. You will experience success in equal measure to what you ultimately have to give.

# Publishing Your Own Book – A Timeline

Self-publishing can be a daunting undertaking. It's easy to be overwhelmed in the process of setting up a publishing company, writing a book, taking care of the business aspects of preparing that book and then there's promotion.

Here's a calendar to guide you in the steps necessary to publishing your book.

## BEFORE WRITING YOUR BOOK

1: **Write a book proposal**. While a book proposal is generally thought of as your foot-in-the-door to a publisher, there's even a greater purpose. As I've pointed out in the article on page 62, a book proposal will tell you if you even have a book. So before sinking your life savings and a year or more of your life into this project, make sure you actually have something worth publishing.

2: **Determine if publishing is for you**. Talk to others who have self-published to find out what it entails. Read about self-publishing. I recommend *The Self-Publishing Manual* by Dan Poynter. Study how a book is marketed. Preparing the book for market is a huge job, but marketing your book is ongoing. The amount of time you put into marketing will relate directly to how successful your book will become.

## WHILE WRITING YOUR BOOK

3: **Name your publishing company**. Be careful about using a name that reflects the nature of your book. You may decide to publish books in different genres in the years ahead. While Lace and Linen Press would be appropriate for a company producing books on sewing or crafts, it doesn't work very well for historical or travel books.

4: **Apply for a Fictitious Business Name**. This is available through your County Clerk. Have two or three names in mind in case your first choice is taken.

5: **Establish a business address**. If you're working out of your home, you might consider signing up for a post office box or a box at a mailbox store to use for business correspondence.

6: **Order business stationary**.

7: **Open a business checking account**.

8: **Request a block of International Standard Book Numbers (ISBN).** Assign one number to each book you publish. This number identifies your publishing company and the book and is necessary for books sold in the retail market. R.R. Bowker is the U.S. agency for distributing ISBN. You cannot purchase just one number. You will probably want to start with a block of ten numbers, however you can also order blocks of one hundred or one thousand. The cost as of this printing is $225 for ten. For more information and to purchase your ISBN printout, visit www.isbn.org. Contact the Agency by phone: 877-310-7333 or email: isbn-san@bowker.com.

9: **Request an Advanced Book Information (ABI) form**. About six months before your book is finished, fill out the form and send it to R.R. Bowker (POB 6000, Oldsmar, FL 34677-6800). This ensures that your book will be listed in *Books in Print*—one of the industry's most important directories. There is no charge for the form or for the listing. *Books in Print* is the directory that bookstores use to locate ordering information about your book when customers request it by name.

10: **Request Copyright forms**. Contact the U.S. Copyright Office at 202-707-3000 or www.loc.gov/copyright. Wait to file this form until after you've completed your work on the book. The cost at this printing is $30.

11: **Contact your State Board of Equalization** and request a resale permit.

## WHEN YOU'RE ALMOST FINISHED WRITING THE BOOK
(About six months before completion)

12: **Assign an ISBN to your book**.

13: **Fill out an ABI form and send it in**.

14: **Order your Publisher's Cataloguing in Publication information (P-CIP).** This information, which is printed on your Copyright Page, is important for library use. Contact Quality Books at 800-732-4450 or visit their Web site at www.quality-books.com. The cost is now $150 for all first editions. And not all requests for P-CIP are accepted.

**WHILE EDITING YOUR BOOK** (About three months before the book is completed)

**15: Search for a printer.** If you're going the traditional printing route, send a "Request for Price Quote" to eight or ten printers and ask to see samples of their work. The printer will want to know quantity of books, number of pages, type of binding, paper stock, size, number and type of illustrations, text color and cover ink (4-color, 2-color?). Find printers listed in your local Yellow Pages, in *Literary Market Place* (in the reference section at your library) and ask for recommendations from other small publishers. If you want to work with a POD company or produce an ebook, research these avenues.

**16: Send pre-publication review copies**. While some experts are now suggesting that the small publisher doesn't have a chance for a review by one of the important pre-publication reviewers, others recommend submitting your manuscript. If you get a review, this could jumpstart your book sales in a big way. I know self-published authors who have had marvelous reviews in these major review publications. Pre-publication reviews appear in magazines that are read by the book industry: bookstore and library buyers, for example. And these reviewers want to see the book before it's published, so don't wait to send a finished book. While you can send your manuscript, you'll make a better presentation if you have it bound even with a plain cover. Give your publication date as anywhere from three to six months in advance. Enclose a cover letter with your galley that includes the title, author's name, publication date, ISBN, name of publishing company, price and contact information. If you have a distributor or wholesaler lined up, list their contact information as well. Generally, however, you don't approach distributors and wholesalers until you have a book to show them. (See a partial list of pre-publication reviewers at the end of this article).

**17: Commission someone to design your cover**. Contact authors and small publishers to find out who designed their covers. Locate graphic artists and illustrators through an organization such as SPAWN, the Yellow Pages or a local arts directory.

**18: Set your price**. There are a couple of ways to figure your price. Some experts suggest pricing your book at an amount eight times the cost per book. This means, if the total cost of producing your book is $5.00 each, you should charge $40 for the book. If you produce an 80-page book for around $1.50, you must charge $12. This doesn't seem logical to me. I recommend comparing the price of books similar to yours to help determine your price.

19: **Order a bar code**. Contact Bar code Graphics, Inc. at sales@bar code-us.com. You will need an ISBN and the price of the book in order for the company to create your bar code. I paid $10 for the bar code for this book through Bar code Graphics as we did the transaction digitally.

## WHEN THE BOOK IS FINISHED

20: **Choose a printing method and a printer**. Find out how they want you to deliver the book and cover design and prepare it this way.

21: **Give the book to the printer.**

## WHILE THE BOOK IS AT THE PRINTER (approximately two to six weeks prior to publication)

22: **Solicit pre-publication orders**. Send announcements to your mailing list which should include everyone who has expressed any interest in your book, friends, family, co-workers and acquaintances. State to those whom you plan to give complimentary copies that they have one coming and if they'd like to order additional copies they may do so. Also mail notices to local libraries, bookstores and anyone interested in the topic. Make it easy for people to order books. When you start receiving orders, don't cash checks until the books have been put in the mail to the customer. Sometimes I offer a discount for those folks who order by a certain date.

23: **Fill out and send the Copyright form.** There's a $30 filing fee.

24 **Create a list of post-publication reviewers.** This might include book reviewers for magazines, newsletters and Web sites on the topic of your book and general book reviewers,

25: **List those to whom you wish to send complimentary copies**. This might include those involved in helping to create the book: cover designer, typesetter and so forth. Prepare promotional packets for key book reviewers and address mailers in preparation for your first shipment.

26: **Start planning your promotion program**. (Read the articles in Chapter Six for marketing tips.)

# AFTER PUBLICATION

27: **Ship and deliver review copies, complimentary copies and pre-publication orders**.

28: **Send two copies of the book to Copyright Office** (address on Copyright form)

29: **Send three copies of the book to the Library of Congress** (address on Copyright form)

30: **Send one copy of the book to Quality Books**. Ask them to consider your book as a distributor to the library market. (1003 W. Pines Road, Oregon, IL 61061-9680)

31: **Fill out paperwork for the State Board of Equalization**.

32: **Apply for a business license**. Check into your city/county requirements for a business license. I have to have a county business license and one for the city since I live (work) in the county and sell books in bookstores in the city.

33: **Contact distributors and wholesalers**. Find listings in *Literary Market Place*.

34: **Put your promotional plan into action**.

## Pre-publication Reviewers

Kirkus Reviews
770 Broadway
New York, NY 10003

Library Journal
245 W. 17 th. St.
New York, NY 10011

American Library Association Booklist
50 East Huron St.
Chicago, Il. 60611-2795

# *Chapter Six*

..............................

## *Book Marketing 101*


♦Market Your Book Before it's a Book


♦10 Ways to Increase Book Sales


♦Market Your Book Without Leaving Your Comfort Zone


♦ Promotion Basics for the Bold and the Bashful


♦Promote Your Book Through Magazine Articles


♦Promote Your Book Through Spin Offs

# Market Your Book *Before* it's a Book

They say that everyone has a book in them. Until recently, however, relatively few people ever put their book on paper. Major advances in publishing technology and easy access to this technology have changed all of that. Now, more and more people worldwide are producing books in all genres.

As a savvy author, you've probably been reading about the publishing trade. By now you know that, in order to sell your book, you must promote it. And this is true whether you're self-published or have a traditional publisher. But did you know that the time to start marketing your book is *before* it's published? Here's how:

**Write a book proposal**. This is your guide to writing and marketing the book. Among other things, an effective book proposal includes a market analysis (your competition) and promotional ideas. The market analysis is particularly important in determining whether there is a market for your book. Check Amazon.com and visit your closest mega-bookstore to find out how many different books there are on your topic. How are they selling? (Read about writing a book proposal on page 62.)

**Make your book salable**. A client once came to me complaining that he couldn't sell his wonderful book. One look and I could see why. The book was not suitable for sale through most bookstores because it didn't have an International Standard Book Number (ISBN) or a barcode. Neither did he fill out the Advance Book Information sheet for RR. Bowker, so his book was not listed in *Books In Print*.

Before producing a book today, do your homework. Find out what is necessary in order to sell your book in the most popular markets.

Most bookstores require the book have an ISBN and a bar code. They reference *Books in Print* for ordering information on books they don't stock. If you expect to tap into the library market, you'll want to order Publisher's Cataloguing-in-Publication information from Quality Books. (Read more about preparing your book for market on page 60)

**Choose an appropriate binding**. Most libraries and bookstores prefer to stock perfect-bound books—books with spines. Some systems won't accept spiral bound or saddle-stitched books.

**Talk about your book everywhere you go**. Even before it's a book, start promoting it to friends, coworkers and people you meet in passing. I recommend that authors come up with a thirty-second commercial—that is a thirty-second spiel describing your book when someone asks about it.

**Line up experts to give testimonials**. Whether you're writing a book featuring rescue dog stories, beauty treatments from the kitchen or 101 summer activities for kids, find a couple of experts in the field to review your manuscript. Use his or her testimonial on your back cover and in your promotional materials. You'll notice that I have included testimonials from ten writing/publishing experts in this book. And I asked another one to write the foreword. It's possible that it was something one of these experts wrote that inspired you to purchase this book.

**Involve a lot of people and organizations in your book**. I'm working on a book about fatherhood and fathering and I've interviewed approximately fifty individuals and heads of related organizations and agencies so far. I plan to list them in the book. Most of these people will want at least one copy of this book. Some of the agencies will probably recommend the book or even distribute it. Others might purchase copies to give away.

**Create a mailing list**. Log names from your Rolodex, Christmas card list, address books and business files. Be sure to add family, friends, neighbors, former neighbors, your children's teachers, coworkers, your yoga classmates, the folks you met on your last cruise and so forth. Keep adding to this list as you continue to meet new people and make new business contacts. While the book is being printed, send pre-publication flyers to this list offering a discount for orders received by a certain date. I paid over half of my printing bill for the 2nd edition of *The Ojai Valley, An Illustrated History* with pre-publication orders.

**Tap into the phone book**. Prior to the publication of my books, I typically spend several evenings gathering names from telephone books for my mailing list. For example, if your topic is healthy grieving, list funeral homes, family counselors, psychologists, doctors and hospice groups that might want to have your book on hand for their clients. Reference telephone directories from other counties and states at your public library or use an Internet telephone directory. Or buy mailing lists from companies that provide them.

**Find your niche market**. Contact specialty storeowners and/or professionals who might make up your niche market. Tell them about your book idea and ask for their input. For the book on rescue dogs, for example, you would contact pet storeowners, veterinarians, pet groomers and animal trainers.

**Create a Web site.** Make it clear on your home page that you have a book to sell and provide easy-to-follow ordering information. List your URL on the cover of your book, your business cards, your letterhead and as a "signature" in all of your emails. (Read more about building a writer's Web site on page 149.)

# 10 Ways to Increase Your Book Sales

The success of your book depends on your willingness to promote it. Following are ten ideas that will surely get the customers' attention.

1. **Market by the season**. You probably intensify your promotional efforts during the Christmas/Hanukah holidays. But do you give any thought to the other seasons? Push gardening and travel books for summer reading and novels during winter when people like to curl up with a good book. I market my Hawaiian luau book for Father's Day in June and my grandparenting book for Grandparent's Day in September. For more seasonal marketing ideas go to: www.dailyglobe.com/day2day.html

2. **Email press releases to newspaper column editors**. Find newspapers listed online at www.newspaperlinks.com or www.newspapers.com. Locate the appropriate editor for your category: cooking and foods, outdoor living, fitness and health, the arts, family or spiritual, for example. Write a brief press release about your book and include your phone number so the editor can call you for an interview.

3. **Make news**. Go out and do something newsworthy. If your book is on dog training, offer to teach volunteers at a local animal shelter to work with the dogs that are waiting for adoption. If your novel features the homeless community, spearhead a program for the homeless. And be sure to tell the press about it.

4. **Target the right audience**. This sounds elementary, but sometimes the best laid plans... I planned to market my book, *Write On! Journal-keeping for Teens,* through public schools and youth organizations. I discovered after publication, however, that it's too spiritually oriented for mainstream educational and youth organizations. My new focus audiences for that book are Christian schools and church youth leaders.

**5. Publish an online newsletter**. If you have several books in the same genre, a business or advocacy group relating to your book and/or an endless supply of information on the topic, consider publishing an online newsletter. Most online newsletters are free and many of them have subscribers numbering the thousands. Karen Stevens advertises her book, *All For Animals*, in her monthly newsletter, which is designed to educate and inform readers on cruelty-free living for animals. Azriela Jaffe is the author of several books. She writes two free monthly email newsletters: one for entrepreneurial couples and the other on creating your own luck. Of course, she mentions her books in each of her very informative and entertaining newsletters.

**6. Create a line of books**. Producing a series of books gives you more credibility in your field. And, it's easier to market books on the same topic. Instead of writing another full-blown book, however, you might offer customers additional or relating material in the form of pamphlets. Publish a small collection of poetry or short stories to accompany your book on writing. Produce booklets featuring various types of crafts and activities for kids to enhance a book on parenting.

**7. Talk about your book everywhere you go**. I've sold books at the baseball field, in line at the grocery store, at my class reunion, while waiting at the doctor's office and even in church. It's not necessary to make a pest of yourself. Just be prepared to talk about your book should the opportunity arise. Just this morning, while at my hairdresser's, I asked if anyone needed autographed copies of my local history book for Christmas gifts this year. I sold four. Contact www.toastmasters.org for information about honing your communication skills.

**8. Give incentives to buy**. Offer a free chapter or two on your Web site or nicely bound as a handout. Give away advertising bookmarks. Package your book with an interactive CD or some other item. I've thought about packaging my Hawaiian luau book with a lei-making kit or uli-ulis (feather gourds). I could include a journal and a pen with my journaling book.

9. **Give Seminars, workshops and demonstrations**. Teddy Colbert, the author of *The Living Wreath*, often demonstrates how to make wreaths from live plants. Debbie Puente is the author of *Elegantly Easy Crème Brulee and Other Custard Desserts*. She frequently gives demonstrations in how to make crème brulee. Do these authors sell books through these events? Absolutely.

10. **Ask for the sale.** Raven West is the author of two novels, *Red Wine for Breakfast* and *First Class Male*. I heard her speak recently on the subject of book promotion and she told the audience that she sells more books when she asks for the sale than when she just sits back and waits for it. Be bold. Say, "Please buy my book." Or "How many copies would you like?" You might be surprised at the response.

# Market Your Book
## Without Leaving Your Comfort Zone

If you're like many authors, you can do without the glare of publicity. You prefer being left alone to collect your royalty checks and write more books. You realize it's necessary to promote your book, but you also want to keep a low profile. You're in luck. I'm the author of *Over 75 Good Ideas for Promoting Your Book* and nearly fifty of them can be implemented without leaving the comfort of your home office. Here's a sampling:

**Send news releases**. Devote an hour each day sending news releases to newspapers in the appropriate regions. Locate contact information in *The Business Phonebook U.S.A., Gale's Directory of Publications and Broadcast Media* and *Ulrich's International Periodicals Directory* (in the reference section at your library). Purchase mailing lists for newspapers and other publications through companies such as Para Publishing (www.parapublishing.com) or *Info USA* (www.infousa.com). Access online newspaper listings at www.newspapers.com

Send news releases initially to announce your new book and periodically to get additional publicity. Link a news release with a season, holiday or event. Refer to *Chase's Calendar of Events* for promotional tie-ins for your book (in the reference section at your library).

**Research new markets**. Continually explore new outlets for your book. Using the tools listed above and others, such as *Literary Market Place, Writer's Market* and the Internet, locate magazines and newsletters that do book reviews and specialty stores that carry books like yours.

**Get involved online**. Explore sites related to the topic of your book. Whether you've written about health, pets, parenting, relationships or grasshoppers, you're bound to find countless sites on that subject.

If the site has a list of recommended books, inquire about adding yours. Offer to write articles for these sites and any accompanying newsletters. Participate in chats.

**Build a Web site and they will come**. Create your own Web site or hire or barter with someone to do it. A student built my site as her class project. She got plenty of experience and a good grade and I got a free site where I can promote my books.

First, visit at least twenty-five sites to determine what features you want. Clarity, simplicity and ease should be your major goals. Make it easy for visitors to buy your books. If you don't want to take credit cards, for example, arrange a link with Amazon.com where consumers can charge their purchase. (See page 149 for a more detailed article on building a Web site.)

**Advertise via email.** Most email services offer customers a "signature." This is a feature that allows you to add a tagline at the end of your emails. You type in the information, such as the title of your book and your Web site address, and it automatically appears at the end of your email messages.

**Do piggyback marketing**. Hopefully, you have developed and are maintaining a good mailing list including friends, relatives, acquaintances, business associates, your plumber, former school teachers, people you've met online, your veterinarian, etc. Continually add to your mailing list and use it whenever you have an announcement to make about your book or you want to remind everyone to consider your book as a gift for an upcoming holiday, for example.

Enhance that mailing list by hooking up with other authors whose books compliment yours and who also have impressive mailing lists. Offer to send their flyers with your marketing pieces and book orders if they will send yours with theirs.

**Donate copies of your book.** Give books for silent or live auctions and as prizes at local events. Leave copies in waiting rooms and corporate lounges. Be sure to include ordering information with each book. You'll be surprised how many people will decide to purchase a copy of their own or as gifts for friends. I've left slightly damaged copies of my books at the local hospital waiting room, in doctor's offices and at my beauty shop, for example.

**Create a contest around the theme of your book**. If you have a book of poetry, run a poetry contest. If you wrote a cookbook, establish a cooking competition. Your publishing company could launch a contest to find the best title for an upcoming book. Advertise your contest through flyers, articles and announcements in relating magazines, newspapers and club and organization newsletters.

**Write a letter to the editor of your local paper or a national magazine**. Read publications and articles related to the topic of your book. Write a letter to the editor when appropriate and identify yourself as the author of (name of your book). Here's an example: I know an author who published a book featuring insect zoos and butterfly exhibits throughout the U.S. She might read an article in *Family Circle* about summer vacation spots designed with kids in mind. This would provide a great opportunity for her to promote her book. She might write a letter to the editor saying, "I loved the article on kid-friendly vacation spots. The only thing missing—and something that would delight my own children—were exhibits related to bugs." She might suggest a couple of good ones and then end by saying that there are hundreds more listed in her book, *Let's Go Buggy*. Just think of the great publicity should they publish her letter.

**Carry your book everywhere you go**. Don't miss an opportunity to talk about your book. Take it with you when you attend business meetings, social gatherings, networking meetings and so forth. If you run into an acquaintance downtown and they ask, "What have you been doing, lately?" bring out your book and show it to them.

# Promotion Basics
## For The Bold and The Bashful

Writers are notoriously reclusive. Most of us work in solitary confinement and we like it that way. When we become authors, we hope to see our books hit the Best Seller list, but we'd rather not get involved with making that happen. What we want is to continue writing. Right?

Unfortunately, this concept is not very realistic. In order to sell your book, you must promote it. And this is true whether you are self-published or have a traditional publisher.

Most publishers today do little or nothing to promote your book. They rely on the author to make sales. In fact, they often accept or reject a manuscript based on the author's willingness and ability to market his own book. How does the publisher know whether or not the author will do the marketing? By studying his or her book proposal.

A book proposal is your guide to writing and marketing the book. An effective book proposal helps you decide if you have a book at all and whether it's marketable. A proposal consists of an overview of the book, a comparison of competitive works, a market potential, a chapter outline, one or two sample chapters and an author bio. (Read more about book proposals on page 62.)

I recently asked Richard O'Connor, then acquisitions editor at Renaissance Books, "How important is the marketing portion of your book proposal when presenting it to a publisher?" He responded, "Critical."

He went on to tell me about one book that his company may have rejected except for the fact that the author had close ties with a large national company that was interested in stocking the book and promoting it. Because of this company's commitment and the author's active involvement in marketing it, they sold 60,000 copies in just over two years.

## Your Promotional Schedule

Time is a major factor in book promotion. If you can't give your book your undivided attention, at least commit to a schedule. Vow to make three contacts per day or spend one or two days every week pursuing marketing efforts.

When Debbie Puente came out with her book, *Elegantly Easy Crème Brulee*, she spent a minimum of two hours every day, five days a week on the phone or sending emails in an effort to drum up new business. She says, "If you make ten contacts a day everyday and get one good lead a day, that's five good leads a week."

Here are some ideas for spending that time effectively:

1. **Contact specialty shops**. Maybe you have a book of stories about vintage airplanes. Rather than relying totally on bookstores, approach hobby shops, toy stores and small airports about carrying your book. A book on planting an herb garden might sell well in home and garden centers, nurseries, flower shops and gift shops.

2. **Schedule book signings**. Every author dreams of his/her first big book signing. Keep in mind, however, that book signings, even in the large bookstores, are as successful as you and the bookstore manager make them. To draw more interest, plan a demonstration or presentation. Debbie Puente often demonstrates how to makes crème brulee at her signings and they are well attended.

Send press releases with a professional photo of yourself to all local newspapers about two weeks before the event. Ask the bookstore manager to display your book and a sign announcing the event during the week before. Send notes or call all of your friends. Contact other authors that you know. Authors, who have sat alone at a book signing, are notoriously supportive of other authors. (For more about book signings, see page 108.)

3. **Promote your book as a premium or incentive item**. Approach local banks or other businesses and offer a discount for quantities of your book as a giveaway to customers. If you mention a product in your book, contact a company that specializes in that product to see if they want to use your book as an incentive or premium item.

4. **Find buyers on the Internet**. The Internet is a virtual goldmine of resources for selling books of every kind. Use search engines to locate sites related to your book topic. Contact the site owner about reviewing your book for their newsletter, creating a link to your site, allowing you to publish an article on their site and/or tap into their message boards. I've sold several copies of my Nordhoff Cemetery book over eBay.

5. **Attend book fairs and shows**. My colleagues and I have found book fairs and shows to be exceedingly successful but only when the author is the one who is touting his or her book. Don't waste your time or money sending your book to an event with someone else. No one else knows your book like you do and no one else cares about it as much as you do.

This is no time to become part of the background. Step forward and show people your book. Talk about it. I know one woman who, when things slow down at her booth, she dons a sandwich board advertising her book and walks around talking to people about it.

6. **Try at least one new marketing technique every month**. Tap into the library market, create a promotional display to offer bookstores and specialty shops where your books are sold  or get added recognition for your book by entering it in contests.

Use the foregoing to develop a personal marketing plan. Express your creativity, assertiveness and persistence and you will surely be either mildly or wildly successful in your endeavors to sell books.

# Promote Your Book Through
# Magazine Articles

The editor of a writing-related ezine said to me the other day, "I don't know why more authors don't offer us articles. We almost always publish them along with their bio. It's great publicity for their books."

Why not promote your book doing what you love best—writing? Here are several examples to help get your started.

Many popular magazines and ezines use book excerpts. Of course, they generally want excerpts from books that relate to their magazine—cooking magazines want excerpts from cookbooks, a travel magazine will quote travel books and poetry magazines want to excerpt poetry books.

Use your imagination to come up with more possibilities. If your book features Native American art in Southern California, for example, a California history or travel magazine might be interested in publishing your chapter on California tribes. An excerpt from a book on tax tips for home-based businesses might provide a good article for a writer's magazine.

Submit articles on topics only remotely related to your book and still promote it. I promoted my journal-keeping book through articles featuring journaling techniques for writers, how to teach journal-keeping in the classroom and journaling as a problem-solving tool for adults. But I can also plug this book even if I'm writing an article about parenting.

I might mention, for example, that when I was writing the journal-keeping book, I met a mother who encouraged her children to journal about issues that came up between them.

I also used articles to promote my book, *The Mainland Luau: How to Capture the Flavor of Hawaii in Your Own Backyard*. There are the obvious articles: "Eight Ways to Roast a Pig," "Recipes for Your Backyard Luau," "Fresh-Flower Lei-Making," "The Family Reunion Luau" and "Tips for Learning the Hawaiian Language." And there are the obscure: how about a piece on early culture comparisons for an ethnic or history magazine; flower arranging for a floral or gardening magazine; examining the lost continent of Lemuria (now the Hawaiian Islands) for a travel, history or New Age magazine or the mechanics of writing a how-to book for a writer's magazine. Do you see how I could promote the luau book in any of these articles?

You can almost always get a tagline at the end of an article. Use this as an opportunity to promote your book. I often write, "Patricia Fry is the author of several books including *Creative Grandparenting Across the Miles: Ideas for Sharing Love, Faith and Family Traditions* (Liguori Publications, 800-325-9521). If the topic of the article more closely relates to the luau book, my journal-keeping book, my writing books, the metaphysical book or one of my local history books, I promote those, instead.

The most effective promotional articles are those relying on your expertise. Most magazine and ezine editors will reject articles that blatantly promote a product, so keep your article from sounding like a sales pitch for your book. Focus on what you can give rather than what you hope to gain. Simply write a useful and informative article suitable to a particular magazine and mention your book where appropriate.

Expect to be paid anywhere from $50 to $1,000 for an article. You might also be asked to give away some of your promotional pieces. And why not, if it means having them published in a national magazine that's read by anywhere from 20,000 to 500,000 people?

By now, you probably have dozens of ideas for marketing your book through articles. To come up with even more:
- Study a variety of magazines from cover to cover.
- List as many topics related to your book as you can.
- Brainstorm with friends and family.

Do articles sell books? I believe so. I've sold dozens of articles based on the luau book and have, as a result made a lot of book sales. Less than a year after self-publishing *The Mainland Luau*, I reprinted it. A year later, my stock was running low again and, because of my good sales record, I had an offer that I couldn't resist from Island Heritage Publishing Company in Hawaii. Now they publish and distribute this book under the new title, *Entertaining Hawaiian Style*.

Writing a book is fun. Promoting it can be terrifying and intimidating. That's why I recommend to authors that they start their book promotion effort doing something they love—writing.

# Promote Your Book Through Spin Offs

What's a *spin off*? It's a by-product or a follow-up to the original. Within the context of a book, it might be a sequel or any number of other writings related to the theme of your book.

The point of a spin off is to generate more sales. Not only will you have additional items to sell, but each book, pamphlet, guide or list that you produce is a marketing tool for the original book.

Let's say that you've written a book on raising healthy children. You might follow up with pamphlets featuring how to develop the habit of exercise in youngsters, good-for-kids snacks, recipes for healthy families or an activity book for kids featuring healthy choices, for example.

Follow a book on growing a kitchen herb garden with one on selling herbs at local farmers markets, how to make herb teas or simple herbal remedies from your backyard.

Spin off books or pamphlets can boost sales for fiction books as well. For example, if your novel depicts life in a small town in Pennsylvania, follow up with a book featuring bed and breakfast inns in that state or create a mystery for readers to solve based on some of the characters in your original book. Maybe you've compiled a book of your poetry. Next, produce a pocket calendar or greeting cards highlighting some of the lines from your best poems.

Plan carefully before launching your spin off. Ask yourself:
> Who is my audience?
> What have my readers asked for?
> Is there something I should have included in my original book?
> How will I distribute the spin off item?
> Is it cost effective to produce another book/pamphlet or other items?

After I produced my 360-page local history book, folks started asking for more. I complied by writing a 55-page booklet featuring the history of the local pioneer cemetery and profiling the earliest burials there. I also wrote an in depth history of one of our oldest private schools. Many of the people who bought the original history book also purchased the other two.

Some authors promote items along with their books. Debbie Puente endorses a culinary torch to accompany her book, *Elegantly Easy Crème Brulee and Other Custard Desserts.* Someone wanting the book will most likely buy the torch, which is used to caramelize the sugar on the crème brulee. And someone with the torch will probably need her book.

Produce a newsletter as a spin off to your book. Azriela Jaffe, who promotes several of her books through two monthly newsletters cautions, however, "I don't think you should write a newsletter just to sell books. The reason to do a newsletter is to position yourself as an expert in your niche, to expand your reach and to give something of value to your customers." Jaffe follows her own advice. While she does sell books through her entrepreneurial couples and creating luck newsletters, she also offers plenty of information and inspiration for her newsletter readers.

Karen Stevens launched a newsletter to support her organization, All For Animals. Her book, *All For Animals,* followed. Stevens' desire is to motivate and inspire people to be more compassionate toward all animals. Not only does her newsletter help in this mission, it gives her a venue for promoting her book. And it puts her in touch with people with compassionate animal stories for her next book.

Give your customers more than they expected. Think about how you feel when you go to the store to buy an avocado, for example, and discover that you can get two for the price of one. Delight your customers by giving them something extra.

Create handouts to package with your book shipments and to give at book signings, book festivals and presentations. I have a scrumptious pork roast recipe that I often give when promoting my Hawaiian luau book. I offer my meditation walking article to folks interested in my metaphysical book, *Quest for Truth*. And I love handing out copies of some of my writing articles when promoting my writing books. Budding authors particularly enjoy my article featuring a self-publishing timeline.

Before thinking about your next book, consider writing a spin off to promote your original book. Sometimes it pays to keep all of your eggs in one basket.

# *Chapter Seven*

. . . . . . . . . . . . . . . . . . . . . . .

## *An Author Wears Many Hats*

♦ **Book Signing Tips for Authors**

♦ **When You're Also the Photographer**

♦ **Your Publicity Photo**

♦ **Writers as Mentors—Bringing Children Along**

# Book Signing Tips For Authors

Once you're over the thrill of holding your latest published book in your hands, it's time to get down to the business of selling it. And a favorite promotional activity for most authors is the book signing.

Contrary to popular belief, people don't typically swarm authors at these events and purchase hundreds or thousands of copies of their books. An unknown author might sell just a handful of books if she's lucky. But, her success rate increases with her efforts. Here are a few dos and don'ts that will help make your next book signing more successful.

1: Don't wait for an invitation. Take the initiative and approach the managers of businesses related to your book topic and local bookstores. Offer to give a presentation or to sign books for their customers.

I sell more books at signings where I give presentations. I like to introduce myself and my book, give a brief overview and then I generally answer audience questions.

If the subject of your book lends itself to demonstrations, plan one for this event. When Swedish animal behaviorist and author, Anders Hallgren talks about his book, *Smoke Alarm Training for Your Dog* (Hallwig Publishing, 2002), he usually brings a dog with him to demonstrate his techniques. California resident, Jean Wade, often serves sugarless desserts during her signings to promote her book for diabetics, *How Sweet It is ... Without the Sugar.*

## 2 ½ weeks before the event:
2: Send Press Releases with a photograph of yourself or your book cover to all newspapers within a forty-mile radius. Relate the particulars of the planned event, write something about your book and include your bio. Give your phone number. An editor may want to contact you for more information.

3: Make calls and send post cards and emails to friends, acquaintances, business associates and club affiliates inviting them to your signing. Post flyers on bulletin boards where you work and in public places. Have notices placed in appropriate company and club newsletters and bulletins.

**Ten days in advance of the event:**
4: Find out if the store plans to design posters and flyers to advertise your signing. If not, do this yourself and deliver them to the store a week in advance of the event. Ask the manager to include a flyer with each purchase during the week prior to your event.

5: Offer to design a store display of your books.

**One week in advance of the event**:
6: Know ahead of time what to expect: Will you have a microphone? Lectern? Table at which to sit? Or will you have to arrange for these things yourself?

7: Make sure the store has enough books in stock.

**The day of the event**.
8: Dress to stand out in a crowd, but not so dramatically as to distract from your presentation.

9: Be prompt. Arriving a little early won't hurt and it will give you time to settle in.

10: Bring handouts—a relating article or a sample chapter, for example.

11: Reach out to people, don't wait for them to come to you. Hand copies of your book to folks in the audience or who visit your signing table. If you're sitting all alone, walk around the store and strike up a conversation with customers. Hand a copy of your book to them. Someone is more apt to purchase something they've held in their hands.

12: Keep track of the number of books you autograph in case there is a discrepancy.

**After the event:**
13: Send a note of thanks to the store manager and staff.

14: Attend other signings and note what works and what doesn't.

15: Arrange more book signings, presentations and demonstrations at bookstores and/or specialty stores. Consider a combined signing with other authors. This should be someone whose book compliments your own, but doesn't compete with it. A book of animal-related poems and a novel about a dog might entice the same buyers. You could promote your book on writing thank you notes along with one featuring how to make paper products. Another compatible combination might be a book on marketing Web site businesses and one featuring how to gear up for a job in technology.

16: Realize that signings and presentations will rarely exceed your expectations and hardly ever meet your highest goals. But *anytime* you are given the opportunity for this sort of free publicity, you are making headway in your promotional effort.

# When You're Also the Photographer

Whether you write nonfiction or fiction, books or magazine articles, you may be called upon occasionally to illustrate your projects with photographs. Of course, you can buy stock photos, you can hire a professional photographer, you can even ask a friend who takes good pictures to do the job for you. Or you can become camera savvy yourself.

My writing interests have always leaned toward nonfiction. When I started writing for publication, I knew it would be beneficial for me to learn how to use a camera. In fact, the first article I pitched required photos. The editor of *Horse and Horseman* loved my idea for an article featuring various ways to use your horse show ribbons. And he asked, "Can you provide us with half dozen color photographs?"

"Yes," I said, while crossing my fingers behind me in case I was spewing a lie. And then I went to work to finally learn the mechanics of the 35mm camera that had intimidated me for so many years. As it turned out, the editor paid me more for the article than he normally would because the photos were so good. As I recall, one of them even landed on the cover of the magazine.

I have since illustrated several books and numerous articles with my own photographs. I've shot photos of kittens, eagles, trail riders, the process of starting new African violet plants from leaves, old buildings, artists at work, an outdoor bookstore, garden areas and close ups of individuals, among other things.

What does it take to become a decent photographer? Here are some tips:

1.  Become familiar with a 35mm camera. Carry it with you, keep it handy and use it often. In this age of digital photography, I also recommend buying a digital camera.

2.  Practice the type of photography you need to accompany the writing you do. I know a poet who produces lovely books of poetry illustrated by her equally lovely photographs. She should

be ever alert and aware of colorful sunsets, pretty scenery and mood shots to use in her upcoming books. I know another woman who does photography to accompany her car racing articles. Of course, she photographs racecars from various angles every chance she gets.

3. Log your collection of photos. Some publications want slides, some want color prints and a few still ask for negatives. But digital photography is the new wave in illustrating magazine articles and books. When you get a box of slides or a package of prints developed, isolate those that you feel are worth publishing, label and file them using a system that works for you. When you get an assignment to write a piece on feeding wild birds from your balcony, you can look through your wild bird photo collection and be ready with a couple of illustrations.

Most of the time it's necessary to do the photography in conjunction with the interview or research. When you are on a photo shoot:

- Know what type of photos the magazine or book publisher wants: black and white or color prints or digital. Many photographers today carry two or even three cameras to accommodate all possibilities.
- Study the style photos used in this particular magazine or wanted by this publisher. Portrait, action, close-up/dramatic? If I'm shooting to illustrate a piece on a cat rescue facility, for example, I might get a close-up of the facility manager with a kitten or cat, a long shot of an aspect of the place, a picture of her and/or volunteers working with kittens in some capacity and maybe a few close shots of the kittens playing, posing or curled up sleeping.
- Take many more shots than you will need. Take two or three pictures at three different settings. Use a flash for some shots and take others without. You want superior photos. And the best way to ensure that is to have many selections.
- Use a digital camera to view your shots immediately.

To send photos:

1: Create a photo legend. First put your name and phone number or address on each of the photos and slides. I put my name and phone number in pencil on the slides and my address label on the back of photos. Number each photo or slide. Avoid writing on the back of photos. This causes an indentation that shows through to the other side.

On your letterhead, write a description of each photo using corresponding numbers. For example, "Photo number 1: A deer grazing in a field of poppies near a Yosemite waterfall. Photo number 2: Arial Jackson of Arlington, Texas helping her son, Richard, with his homework."

2: Send photos with care. Technology gives us great options for preserving photos digitally. You can use a digital camera and email the picture. You can scan a color or black and white photo and email it. If you are required to mail photos, put slides in a small box, wrap in bubble wrap and send in a larger box. Mail photos and/or negatives in stiff cardboard mailers so there is no chance of the package bending. The post office, mailbox shops, camera stores and photo developing shops have appropriate mailers for photographs

I must point out one danger in becoming an accomplished photographer. This new hobby could begin competing with writing for your creative attention. Since I started forcing myself to learn photography, I've become quite enamored with the process. I belong to a camera club. I enter my photos in contests. I enjoy using my camera almost as much as I enjoy writing. And I find that it is a wonderful creative outlet. Often, when I'm on the verge of writers' burnout, I take my camera outside and start looking for caterpillars to photograph or I snap pictures of the birds at the feeders or in the birdbath. When I really need to shift gears, I take my camera out to nearby Lake Casitas and do some photography while getting my exercise walking around the lake.

# Your Publicity Photo

Whether you freelance for magazines, do business writing, edit clients' work, present writing workshops or are about to publish a book, you need a good publicity photo.

Photos are especially important in this age of technology, when so much of our business is conducted with people we've never met. Today, our Web site is our calling card and our handshake. And your photo on your Web site, your PR material or the cover of your book is your personal greeting. Sometimes your photo can be the deciding factor in getting a job or making a sale.

How often do you turn a book over to look at the author's photo before making the purchase or reading the book? When you need more information about someone who is going to present a seminar or who is offering their professional services, don't you want to see what he or she looks like? You have to judge for yourself whether this is someone you can relate to and respect.

While a photograph can't measure your credibility or express the depth of your personality, this is how many people will initially assess you. When they can't meet you face-to-face, your photo will help them determine whether or not they like you.

If you are a writing professional, you probably need photos for some or all of the following:
- Your Web site.
- Promotional brochures.
- The cover of your published books.
- Flyers advertising your workshops and seminars.
- Magazine editors who want to run your photo with your story.
- Press releases when promoting your book or announcing receipt of an award.

Don't just ask a neighbor to take your picture while posing in the backyard. Put some thought into the image you want to portray and hire a professional to capture that image. Here are some guidelines to note when planning your photo shoot.

### 1. Determine what you hope to achieve through your photograph.

Do you want people to read your book, trust your words, hire you as an editor or sign up for your seminar, for example? Create an appearance that makes an appropriate visual statement. Dress for your photo as you would for a book signing, when meeting with a client or while leading a workshop.

Avoid fabrics in distracting patterns and colors. Instead, choose solid colored clothing or something with a muted pattern in shades that are complimentary and that provide a good contrast to your complexion. If you're a woman, wear a tailored blouse or a suit jacket. To avoid a rigid image, use soft fabrics and light to medium bright colors. Men can dress up in a suit and tie or dress down in a pullover sweater, for example.

We all have many sides to our personalities. Which one of yours do you want to reveal to your particular audience? If you have written a book for children, you may want your publicity photos to depict you as friendly, fun and nurturing. For the cover of a book for the business community, you'll want to appear more professional, confident and poised

It might help to generate the proper demeanor if you stage your photo session amidst your audience of choice. Have the photographer shoot you while interacting with a group of children, for example, or just before or after participating in a business meeting.

### 2. Avoid being too cutesy or too arrogant.

Have you seen those photos of women resting their chins or their cheeks on their hands? This is a precious pose for children, but it's rather silly for a grown woman. Yet, some photographers still use those poses in their repertoire.

Reject photos that make you appear arrogant or that give you a look of superiority. You know the posture I'm talking about—his arms are crossed in front of him and he's smugly looking down his nose at you. He may be the nicest man around, but a photo like this can depict him as a real snob. Lean slightly forward and think happy thoughts while being photographed. You'll come across as more likable.

A couple of years ago, I had an appointment to interview a woman for an article on spiritual healing. She sent me a review copy of her book on this topic. When I received the book, I turned it over, of course, to take a look at her photo. I was shocked. Pictured here was a woman who looked ill. She was dressed in what appeared to be an old sweatshirt, she had no makeup on and her hair didn't look as if it had been washed lately. She had no spark or life light showing through in her photograph. Upon seeing this dreadful photograph, I lost all interest in reading her book and I even canceled our interview.

### 3. Use props with caution.
While shots of you sitting at your desk or standing before an audience at a seminar are okay for some publicity purposes, I suggest that you also have plain headshots on hand.

If you want to generate a sense of warmth in your photo, pose with your cat or dog. It's hard to dislike someone who expresses genuine caring for a pet. Again, I suggest choosing one good shot with your pet and one plain headshot for when you need something more straightforward.

### 4. Hire a professional photographer.
A professional generally has experience in helping people portray the image they want to present. Ask the photographer for advice on what to wear, how to achieve the personality you want represented and so forth

Have someone help you choose from your proofs. Make sure this is someone who knows you and who has some knowledge of public relations.

Order several copies of your favorite shot(s) in 4 x 5 color glossies. If possible, either scan the photo into your computer or have professional pictures taken with a digital camera as well. I receive requests for ten times the digital photos as I do regular photographs.

## 5. Occasionally refresh your photos.

Consider having new photos taken every five or ten years or whenever your appearance has undergone a dramatic change. Sit for new photos if you lose a lot of weight or change your hair color or style, for example.

Just as you would in person, make a good impression the first time and every time through your publicity photos.

# Writers as Mentors
## Bringing Children Along

Most writers develop their passion for writing early in life. Those I've interviewed often tell me, "I've been writing since I could hold a pencil." Or "I can't remember ever not wanting to write." And this is probably true of some of the children that you know.

Did you yearn to be a writer even as a child? Did you have a writing mentor when you were growing up? Do you remember someone in your family encouraging your talent or a teacher challenging you to write? When I posed this question to one writer I know, he said, "I don't recall anyone ever understanding my excitement about writing as I was growing up. I remember trying to write after going to bed at night and my parents telling me to stop playing around and get to sleep."

Another friend had a very different experience. She says, "My father loved to write, but he never got the chance to live his dream. So when he recognized my passion for writing, he encouraged me all the way. I just wish he'd lived to see my first published book."

If you know a child with an interest and/or a talent for writing, you can make a difference in his or her life. How? Get involved.

- Become a formal mentor either in person or online. There are lots of young people out there just waiting for someone to guide them in their writing efforts.
- Respond to those children and youths you meet who have a talent and/or an interest in writing. Offer to read their works and give constructive criticism. Help them to get published.
- Invite the child to attend a book signing or hear a speaker on the genre he/she is interested in.
- Take a child to book festivals where he/she can meet authors.
- Start a writing group for children in your neighborhood.
- Offer to teach a creative writing class through the recreation department.

f you are already involved with a youthful budding writer, here are some
deas for helping them along.

- Give the child assignments to complete and then discuss what makes the work good and how it could be made better. Try completing assignments together. There is an assignment each month in the *Writer's Digest Magazine*, for example.
- Search out online writer's groups and writing opportunities for kids.
- Find books on writing for kids. Give him/her a copy of *A Young Writer's Handbook* by Patricia Fry (Matilija Press, 2003)
- Sponsor the child in a writing contest.
- Encourage him or her to enter a writing project in local contests or for display at the county fair.
- Help kids design and compose greeting cards for special occasion: Mother's Day, birthdays, etc.
- Print their story and bind it as a surprise for the child. Or frame their poem and give it to them as a gift.

Children are our future. Give one or several of them a boost by offering the help you either had or wish you had as a child. It's a win-win situation.

Resources for youth mentors:
NetMentors (www.netmentors.org)
Amazing Kids (www.amazing-kids.org)

# Chapter Eight

·····································

*Hone Your Communication and Networking Skills*

♦ Networking Tips for Authors

♦ Why Writers Need Other Writers

♦ May I quote you? Tips for Successful Interviews

♦ Talk it Up: Hone Your Public Speaking Skills

♦ The Art of Conversation Through Small Talk

# Networking Tips for Authors

Networking is a technique of connecting with other people for the purpose of exchanging ideas and information. It's a fundamental tool in business and can be enormously beneficial to a writer who is looking for work or promoting his or her book. Successful networking takes effort and a willingness to reach out. Following are tips to help you hone your networking skills.

- **Seek out the obvious sources first.** When you need information or input, start by contacting those who should have that information. Call an editor if you need advice on word usage, for example, or a self-published travel writer if you have a question about marketing your book of day trips.

- **Keep detailed Rolodex or database listings**. When you add a name to your Rolodex or learn something new about someone already listed, make a note. Note that this person is a photography buff or that she's a volunteer at a wildlife rehabilitation center. The next time you need a photographer or a good story idea, you'll know where to turn.

- **Network everywhere you go**. Explore potential avenues of information during social and business events, while chatting with a clerk at the grocery store, during parents' night at your children's school or at a book festival, for example.

- **Let it flow naturally**. Networking doesn't have to be forced conversation. Simply watch for the opportunity to talk about your project and take it. Recently, at a time-management workshop, participants were asked to share current projects that seemed to be stalled. One woman announced that she was having trouble finding recruits for her pet therapy program. She signed up two new volunteers that day.

- **Ask and you will receive.** Be specific. Instead of asking a fellow author, "What does marketing a book involve?" say, "What has been your most successful marketing strategy?"

- **Be heads up**. A good networker will be alert to information he can use even when he's not in network mode. Recently, I was telling a fellow Toastmaster about an article I was writing on healing and therapeutic gardens. He told me about his brother-in-law who operates a community garden for the homeless—an unexpected and unsolicited lead that gave my article an additional dimension.

- **Be patient.** Networking can take time. You might talk to a dozen people without locating the information you seek only to have one of them come back weeks later with a lead.

- **Listen, listen, listen.** Successful networkers are good listeners. Sometimes the pearl of information you seek is imbedded in a long, boring explanation.

- **Request additional resources.** Before leaving a networking conversation, always ask for additional references and referrals. When I interview someone for a magazine article, I always ask, "Do you know someone else I might contact?"

- **Avoid feeling obligated**. Not every idea, opinion or bit of information given is useful. Don't feel obligated to use it just because you asked for it.

### Networking Etiquette

- **Respect the time and space of others.** When you approach someone at a meeting or call her to discuss something specific, be considerate of her time. If you need more time, offer to see her professionally or take her to lunch.

- **Do the legwork**. Never ask someone else to make follow-up calls or do additional research for you. Do this work yourself.

- **Be gracious**. Sometimes you'll disagree with the information given or you'll have already tried the suggested procedure. Don't make this an issue. Simply thank the person for his/her help and move on.

- **Offer feedback.** People like knowing when they've been helpful. Call or send a note of thanks and describe how the information given was used

## Tips for the Networkee

Sometimes it's harder to be on the giving end than the receiving end of networking—a problem that it is in your best interest to change.

- **Sow and you shall reap.** If you're reluctant to give, you probably won't get much back. Avoid judging every connection by its money-making potential. Be available without expectation. You will be rewarded.

- **Share even without invitation**. Whenever you become aware of data or a contact that you feel someone can use, offer it.

- **Give with no strings attached.** Give and then let go without attempting to dictate how the information or advice should be used.

- **Know when to say "no."** If someone is pressuring you for more information than you are comfortable giving or attempting to take more time than you have available, suggest they make an appointment for a consultation and then quote your fees. Often people ask me "How do you self-publish a book?"—a question that's impossible to answer in 100 words or less. I've learned to respond within three minutes by giving an overview of the complexities of self-publishing, listing the basic reference materials and offering my services as a publishing consultant.

- **Avoid giving until it hurts**. After responding to a question or sharing information, let the networker do his/her own homework.

Networking can be fun. It's an exciting way to discover new ideas. And it's a viable method of finding the resources and information you need in order to achieve your personal and professional goals.

# Why Writers Need Other Writers

Writers typically enjoy spending time alone, contemplating a plot, developing characters and writing stories or articles in peace and quiet. If we need momentary companionship throughout our writing day, we turn to our feline friends. For cats do not interfere, nor are they critical.

Like many of my colleagues, I once avoided meeting other writers. When I did succumb to a friend's pleas of, "You've got to meet Diane. She's a writer. The two of you have so much in common," I was usually disappointed. We'd exchange the typical "Hello. Nice meeting you. What do you write?" And that's where the conversation stopped. Soon we'd both be looking around for someone with whom we could actually carry on a meaningful conversation.

Worse, however, was trying to talk about the writing life with non-writers. Few people understood my passion for writing. Even those close to me didn't take my career seriously, at first. To most people, a writer is someone who sits down when inspiration strikes and writes for pure pleasure. They don't think of words as salable items. In fact, most non-writers have never met a professional writer.

The more I wrote, the more known I became (at least locally). Soon a flurry of would-be and wanna-be writers were knocking at my door. They wanted to know, "How can I get started as a writer?" "How do I find a publisher for my book?" "Would you critique my first three chapters?" and so forth. As I responded to their questions, I began to realize the value of the information I'd gathered over the years. So I organized that information and developed a workshop which I presented for several years.

That workshop led to my association with Mary Embree and together, we organized SPAWN.

During the five years that the three Chapters of SPAWN met, I attended nearly 200 meetings. And I discovered something interesting. The more I interacted with other writers, the more I benefited. Finally, I felt validated as a writer. I now had other models to follow in carving out my writing career. I was learning things I couldn't learn while working in solitude. And I was able to share the fruits of my own experiences and knowledge with others.

Now, my best friends are writers and my favorite activities are those involving writers. Consequently, my career continues to evolve and I am even more fulfilled as a writer.

Following are some of the advantages of belonging to a writers' organization either online or face-to-face:

**1: It's validating**. You will be interacting with people who understand your passion for writing and your commitment to your profession. Validation is important to writers who sometimes question their decision to write. There were times when I lost confidence in my ability to earn a living as a writer. In fact, on three different occasions, I gave up on writing and took a regular job. The support of other writers helps boost your confidence and keep you focused.

**2: It's motivating**. Spending time in the company of other writers is stimulating. Maybe you're bordering on burnout or suffering from writer's block. Positive conversation with fellow writers can give you a fresh perspective and motivate you to get back to productive work.

**3: It's educational**. I don't recall ever attending a writing-related meeting or participating in a writers' forum without learning something new. Each of us is a teacher and a student. We can learn from the fledgling writer as well as from the seasoned author.

**4: It's a great networking opportunity**. Networking with other writers can benefit your writing business or career. I know an editor who acquires many of her clients through the contacts she makes at writers' events. I met both my page-layout artist and cover designer at writers' workshops. Network with other writers to find a publisher, get marketing ideas, learn how others discipline themselves to work and so forth.

**5: It's inspirational**. When you spend time in the company of other writers, you will become inspired. If you see others achieving their goals, it encourages you to accomplish your own.

Writing groups and online forums have inspired some of my best work. I've sold four articles to *Writer's Digest* based on ideas that came from SPAWN members. The following article topics have also been inspired by some of my SPAWN experiences: how to become a more effective public speaker, how to organize your workspace, networking, how to conduct small talk and a 3500-word piece featuring the modern day writer.

**6: You have the opportunity to give back.** It feels good to offer budding writers some of the fruits of your experience.

If you're a writer who doesn't believe that you need other writers, I urge you to reconsider. Join a writers' group or organization. Participate in an online forum with other writers. But remember that you will get out of the experience what you are willing to put into it.

# May I quote you?
# Tips for Successful Interviews

If you aspire to write magazine articles or nonfiction books, you will probably be required to conduct frequent interviews. Sure, it's easier to write what you know. But if you want to add interest and credibility to your work, you really must tap into the perspective and expertise of others.

When covering an event or reporting on a new concept or trend, get the complete picture by talking to those involved.

Let's say that you're writing about obesity in children. After you've given your views and reported on current findings, turn to the experts. Enhance your article by interviewing the directors of innovative fitness programs in schools throughout the U.S. Talk to the principals of those schools, a few of the parents and a couple of doctors who specialize in childhood obesity. Now you have the makings of an article.

I'm currently working on a piece featuring women who work with animals. I'm in the process of interviewing a woman who spends practically her entire day monitoring two-dozen feral cat colonies, a woman who rescues wild horses and provides a sanctuary for them and another woman who finds homes for abandoned and abused dogs.

If you're timid about approaching experts or have trouble asking the right questions, here are some tips to help you conduct more successful interviews.

1: **Locate experts**. Find professionals and other individuals who can add credibility and anecdotes to your article. While you will probably interview local people for a local publication, a national magazine usually requires representation from across the U.S. In this case, I try to interview someone from the eastern portion of the United States, the western region and somewhere in between. (For more about locating experts, see page 145.)

I also contact more people than I think I will need for the article. Why? Because not everyone is available on my time schedule and not everyone provides the information and quotes I require. If I want to quote three people, I might contact five—or at least have five names lined up to contact.

Sometimes your experts are as close as your own family or circle of friends. When I write something on parenting, I often get the perspective of one of my daughters, for example. When it's a thought-provoking article, I sometimes invite friends to a brainstorming session to help me flesh it out.

2: **Learn something about the experts**. Know your experts' background and their association with the topic before approaching them. If she's an author, read her bio on the book cover or on her page at Amazon.com. If he's a business owner or a politician, call his office and request an information packet.

3. **Write a list of questions**. I try to stick with less than ten specific questions. Four or five of those will usually require some discussion.

Base your questions on this person's quotes appearing in books and articles. Ask open-ended questions. Instead of "Are you looking forward to retirement?" ask, "What will you miss most about working and why?" Instead of "Were you sad when your kids all went away to college?" ask, "How did you feel when you watched your last child leave for college?"

4: **Make contact**. Call or email the interviewee and briefly introduce yourself. Name the magazine you're representing, explain the focus of your article and invite him or her to participate. If they're willing, ask for a telephone interview appointment preferably within the next few days.

Sometimes the interviewee will suggest that you do the interview on the spot. So be prepared with your questions.

I can record telephone interviews. I always ask for permission, however. If the interviewee is hesitant, I explain that I want to be sure to quote him accurately.

If the subject wants to schedule the interview for another day, I let him know how much time we'll need—generally fifteen to twenty minutes. I double check which time zone he's in, so I will make the call at the appropriate time. And I offer to email him or her the questions ahead of time so they are prepared.

5: **Suggest an email interview**. This has become my favorite way to interview. There is no transcribing involved. And most people are willing to participate in an email interview because they can think about their responses and write them out at their leisure. Poor or slow typists, however, generally prefer to speak by phone. Some people think better while speaking than typing.

The downside to the email interview is that sometimes people will procrastinate right past your deadline. And, when doing an email interview, you usually have to send some follow-up questions for clarity and depth.

6: **Ask for clarity**. If you don't understand something, say so. If you need an explanation, ask for it.

7: **Encourage anecdotes**. Articles become more colorful and interesting when sprinkled with anecdotes. Ask the expert to give an example of someone who is unhappy in retirement or who was well prepared for the empty nest.

8: **Confirm personal information**. Verify the correct spelling of the interviewee's name and ask how he or she would like to be credited. Often an expert/author will want their latest book mentioned in the article. If the subject is a professor at a college, you'll want to note that correctly. And some individuals prefer to remain anonymous. Most, not all, magazines will honor anonymity or a pseudonym.

9: **Ask for more**. Before leaving an interview, always quickly request more information. Say, for example, "Can you recommend additional material that might help me with this project?" or "Is there anyone else that I should speak with on this topic?"

10: **Send a copy of the article to participants**. Only if the information is personal or highly technical, will I send a copy of the article to an interviewee *before* publication. But, along with a thank you note, I always send a copy of the published article to everyone who participated.

# Talk it Up!
## Hone Your Public Speaking Skills

You can't sell a book that no one knows about. You won't get writing jobs unless people are aware of your writing skills and services. One way to spread the word is to go out and talk about it.

I tell authors, "Talk about your book everywhere you go." Debbie Puente does this and regularly makes sales. She says, "I sell books at the ball park, the grocery store… Everywhere I go, I sell books." And sometimes she doesn't even have to bring up the subject. When flying home after a book signing in another city, for example, she often walks onto the plane carrying the large sign that advertised her book signing. People notice the sign, realize she's an author and start talking to her. The next thing you know, Puente is autographing books for her fellow passengers.

A writer/author should also be relatively comfortable as a public speaker. I've sold many books and have received great exposure from my numerous public speaking presentations. I speak at civic club and organization meetings, before elder hostel groups and in public schools. I've spoken before numerous writing/publishing groups and I was keynote speaker at officer training for Toastmasters a few years ago. And then there are book signings. While generally, you're simply expected to chat with customers, sometimes authors are required to give informal presentations.

If public speaking gives you noodle knees and sweaty palms, I recommend:

- Join a Toastmasters Club. Go to www.toastmasters.org or call, 800-993-7732 for the one nearest you.
- Join an organization of your choice and gain speaking experience by participating in meetings.
- Get involved with a storytelling group.
- Hire a voice coach. (They are generally listed under music teachers.)
- Observe other speakers. Note what techniques work and which ones don't.

- Take on leadership roles at work.
- Find a mentor—someone who's speaking abilities you admire.

Here are some specific public speaking tips to get your started:

**Speak out**. Many inexperienced orators speak too softly or they allow their voices to drop toward the end of their sentences. Practice speaking up and speaking out. Whether addressing a large audience or a small group, always speak so that you can be heard even in the back of the room.

**Repeat audience questions.** When someone asks a question during your presentation, always repeat it before answering it. This ensures that everyone hears it.

**Make eye contact**. Move your attention around the room as you speak, making eye contact with each person.

**Don't apologize.** Avoid sabotaging your presentation by making excuses for not being well prepared or for having poor speaking skills. This will only direct attention away from your talk. Stand tall, appear self-assured and you will gain the confidence of the audience.

**Handle notes and props effectively**. Avoid focusing too much on your notes while speaking or shuffling through a stack of papers. If you must use notes or props, practice working with them so that this activity doesn't detract from the message of your presentation.

**Use vocal variety**. Make your talks more enjoyable by employing an assortment of vocal tones and pitches rather than speaking in monotone. If you need help developing vocal variety, practice reading to children. Use your highest and lowest voice and everything in between.

**Eliminate non-words**. Inexperienced speakers generally use a lot of filler words such as uh, ah, um, er and so forth. Most of us aren't even aware that we're doing this until someone points it out to us. This is why Toastmasters clubs have an "ah counter" at every meeting—someone who

133

counts the number of filler words each member uses. Find out if your speech is littered with filler words by taping your presentation. Once you become aware that you're using filler words, you can begin working to get rid of them.

**Eliminate poor speaking habits.** Rid your vocabulary of stagnant verbiage. Break yourself of those mundane phrases you like to repeat, such as, "yada, yada, yada" or "know what I mean?" Likewise, watch the overuse of words like "really." Saying "I was exhausted." is a stronger sentence than saying, "I was really exhausted." You can explain how exhausted you were by saying, "I was exhausted beyond anything I'd ever experienced before," or "I was so tired I could have slept for a month."

**Be prepared.** You will be more at ease if you know what to expect upon arrival at the presentation hall. Find out if there will be a lectern or microphone, for example. How many people do they expect? How will the room be set up?

**Know your audience**. And gear your speech to the needs and interests of this particular audience. When I talk about the local history, I give a completely different talk to students at local elementary schools than I do when addressing civic organizations. And my talks to historic society members or local historic preservation commissioners varies from those I give to people visiting our community with an Elder Hostel group, for example.

Anyone can get up in front of an audience and speak. How well you do it is what counts.

# The Art of Conversation
# Through Small Talk

Small talk is the most commonly used form of human communication available to us. Most people, however, consider this sort of casual conversation a waste of time. They think of small talk as shallow, mechanical, meaningless chatter.

What these people don't know is that effective managers, dynamite marketing personnel and other accomplished communicators often begin their more successful and productive conversations with small talk.

A period of small talk before a business meeting helps you:
- Build confidence.
- Learn something about the other person.
- Establish a sense of unity.
- Set the mood for a discussion.
- Gain support for your idea.
- Create a bridge to more meaningful dialogue.

## How Small Talk Benefits You
Small talk is a natural prelude to any serious discussion. It provides you and everyone else involved the opportunity to size up and evaluate the situation.

Even animals in the wild take this "look before you leap" approach prior to getting down to business. When an animal comes upon an unfamiliar situation, territory or another animal, for example, it moves toward and around it very slowly—carefully checking things out before becoming involved.

Small talk is the human's way of sensing a situation before jumping in, but its effectiveness is not just in the words you use. Small talk is most effective when your other senses are also on alert.

Through small talk, you can:

- Put people at ease while creating a smooth transition from the initial greeting to the business at hand. Diving into a business discussion without a preamble makes people uncomfortable and results in a more strained interaction.
- Persuade people to be more receptive to your ideas.
- Encourage others to reveal aspects of themselves.
- Initiate professional opportunities in situations even outside the structure of the business setting.

## Tips for Success

To be successful at small talk, however, you must have something to say. Here are some suggestions:

- Be informed. Read newspapers and watch television news. The daily news is an excellent conversation starter and, by staying informed, you'll always have something of value to say.
- Be prepared with topics useful to your cause or interest. Maybe you're looking for someone to interview for an article about home-based businesses or you're trying to find a page-layout expert. Small talk is a natural networking opportunity.
- Practice speaking on a variety of random topics. Get together with friends and take turns speaking off the cuff.
- Develop a list of topics you're comfortable talking about.
- Ask questions. If someone is speaking on a subject that you know little about, ask and learn.
- Find out about the other person. Those who are most admired for their small-talk skills are those who encourage others to talk about themselves.
- Locate common ground. Does this person share an interest in writing, boating, country music, woodworking, bicycling or hiking, for example? Is she a grandmother? Is he from your home state? Become clever at discovering little commonalities with the people you meet.
- Give and take. Don't monopolize the conversation.
- Listen so it shows. Listening is at least as important in small talk as speaking. Demonstrate a sincere interest in what the other person has to say. It could make the difference between a successful business transaction and a failed one.

- Expect to learn. Look at small talk as an opportunity to learn something new. Learn by being interested in what the other person has to say.

## Topics to Avoid

When small talk is frivolous, meaningless and ineffective, it isn't the fault of small talk, but rather the purveyor of the small talk. As with any form of communication there are taboos. Avoid the following in small talk:

- Go-nowhere topics. Until you become proficient at changing the subject or leading the conversation, avoid topics like traffic or the weather.
- Big topics that go on and on and on. Keep small talk small by avoiding subjects that require wordy explanations. Learn to put otherwise lengthy dissertations in a nutshell.
- Controversial subjects. Stay away from politics, religion and related issues with people whose opinions you don't know, particularly in business settings.
- Clichés. Try to avoid repeating the old tried and over-tried phrases that pop out of our mouths automatically during small talk opportunities.
- Criticism. When you don't know the person you're talking to, don't criticize anyone else. The "over dressed hag" across the room might be his wife. The "back-stabbing overachiever" may be her favorite nephew.

## Improve Your Small Talk Skills

Once you understand the importance of small talk, you'll be much more aware of what takes place during these casual conversations. Here's how to improve your skills:

- Practice, practice, practice—with friends, family members, store clerks, strangers at the bus stop, etc.
- Join organizations where you receive training in speaking: Toastmasters, for example. Or enroll in a class or seminar in communication or interpersonal relationships.
- Socialize. Accept more invitations, join a trade organization or club that is in line with one of your hobbies or interests. Or go out and mingle in public places. Being with strangers who have similar interests provides the perfect arena for small talk opportunities.

## Make a Smooth Transition

When small talk is a prelude to business, it will be necessary at some point to draw it to a close and begin the meeting. The best way to do this is through a purposeful transition. Learn to recognize good transitional points in the process of small talk by watching television talk-show hosts in action. Most of them have impeccable timing and great style in making transitions. Here are a few suggestions:

- Learn to lead. Although knowing how to follow is vital to successful small talk, leading is equally important, particularly when the transition depends on you.
- Recognize an opening and jump in. Say: "Let me tell you what we're going to do in the interview." Or "Shall we get on with the meeting?"
- Stop monopolists in their tracks. If possible wait for them to take a breath or to pause. Then break in with a comment about their topic and immediately lead the conversation in the direction that you want it to go.

## *Chapter Nine*

..........................

## *Getting Down to Business*

♦ **Bookkeeping Tips for Writers**

♦ **Recession-proof Your Writing Business**

♦ **Research Techniques for Writers**

♦ **Develop a Successful Writer's Web Site**

# Bookkeeping Tips for Writers

If you're a freelance writer, an effective record-keeping system is essential. Whether you write letters and design brochures for businesses, collect fees and royalties for books or write articles for magazines, it's imperative that you establish a workable technique of documenting business transactions.

I'm certainly no expert in the field of finance, but I've created a method of record-keeping that has worked for me these past thirty years.

I establish columns in a ledger for tracking query letters. I log the date sent, name of magazine and title or subject of the article proposed. I leave space to log the editor's response which generally amounts to such notations as, "yes," "no," "holding," "out of business," "bad address," or "resubmit in 6 months."

My article ledger is similar only, instead of using one line for each entry, as I do in the query log, I allow four to six lines of space. Here, I write the date the article was requested, date sent, name of magazine, name of article, whether or not it was a reprint or an original and I leave a space for the editor's response, payment date/amount and any additional notes. In the remaining space, I might log the date I sent requested photos, the signed contract or a rewrite. I note whether I sent the article via email or USPS and the proposed date of publication. The more information I record, the easier it is to trace an article or to respond to an editor when he claims he didn't receive the photographs, for example.

Data pertaining to book queries, proposals and manuscripts are also logged in these ledgers.

I keep track of payments received on a separate page in one of the ledgers. These entries include date of payment, date the article appeared, name of magazine, name of article and amount paid. This is what I use to report my article earnings at tax time. This is also where I log royalty payments. I highlight these entries to distinguish them from other monies received because royalties are handled differently on the tax return.

I keep a separate ledger for each of my self-published books with pages designated for book sales, books shipped with payment due, promotional books, inventory and separate pages for regular customers (local bookstores and gift shops, for example).

More editors are accepting queries and article submissions via email. But for those times when you send a query or a manuscript through the mail, always be sure to enclose a self-addressed-stamped envelope (SASE).

Here's a tip that simplifies the task of bookkeeping: Write the date on the back of your SASE as you tuck it into the envelope with your query. When it comes back with either an article request or a rejection slip, you can match the date on the return envelope to the "date sent" entry in your log for quick reference.

This year, I've added a new dimension to my bookkeeping system. I've entered the information from my query and article ledgers into a computer database where I can view the history of an article or a magazine at the touch of the keyboard. I can see at a glance which magazines I've already queried regarding a particular article, which queries have been rejected or accepted by a particular magazine and who still owes me money for articles completed, for example.

A professional freelance writer also needs to keep track of expenses. My method is to save receipts in a file folder and tally them up at the end of the year. Collect receipts for postage and shipping costs pertaining to your business, office supplies, your Internet server and Web host, stationery, books and magazines purchased for educational and research purposes, long-distance telephone expenses that are not covered by the magazine, computer and other office equipment purchases and repairs as well as membership in writing-related organizations.

Keeping good records is not only important at tax time, it's vital to the success of your writing business.

# Recession-Proof
# Your Writing Business

(Written shortly after 9/11/01, but relevant whenever the economy takes a tumble.)

Nearly everyone is concerned about the state of the economy and most of us will be affected by the downturn. It seems unfair that, at a time when writers have so much to say, publishers are producing fewer books and magazine editors are printing fewer stories.

Business drives magazines. When business revenues wane, workers are laid off and advertising slows. Without advertisers, editors can't afford to pay writers. Within the past several months, five of my mainstay magazines have gone under and several others have cut back on the amount of freelance work they're using. Several months ago, one editor, who liked my work, generously assigned me six articles—one each for the next six issues. When I completed the job, the editor wrote an apologetic letter saying that their advertisers were pulling out and they had to cut back on the number of articles they can use in each issue. Over the next eight months, they published two of the six with a promise to use the others as space allows. This magazine has since gone out of business.

In times like these, more editors request articles on spec rather than issuing a contract. They don't know what direction their publication will go in the uncertain economy and they don't want to make any promises they can't keep. Consequently, the writer is often left writing for naught.

What's a writer to do in times of economic struggle? The strategy I use is to rethink and reorganize my business. Adopt the attitude that, if things aren't going your way, find another way. Here are some ideas to help keep your writing business afloat even during the hard times:

- Woo your long-standing clients and editors. Stay in touch with them so they'll think of you when they need something done. Remind them of your skills and make a few suggestions for projects that you might do for them.

142

- Write about the things people need to know during times like these: how to live on less, stress reduction, healthy grieving, penny-saver vacations, quick and easy money-making tips, survival techniques, how to plant a Victory Garden and easy and inexpensive Christmas gifts to make, for example.
- Subscribe to several online and print writing magazines and newsletters. Many of them list jobs for writers while also keeping you updated on trends in the writing industry.
- Go outside your comfort zone. Search out new magazines, ezines, Web sites and businesses that might need your expertise. Browse magazine racks at bookstores and study *Writer's Market*, for example.
- Take on clients. There are always people wanting help writing, editing or self-publishing a book or researching their family history. Become their paid mentor.
- Produce pamphlets to market through appropriate agencies and or/businesses—recipes for heart patients, how to keep the faith when the world seems doomed or how to garden away arthritis pain, for example.
- Do something entirely different. Teach writing through a local adult education program, write ads for businesses, typeset manuscripts for clients, conduct research for others or scour the Web looking for those sites that need help with spelling and grammar and then apply for the job.
- Write for less. As one writer friend says, "When times are tough, I'm never above any writing assignment no matter how superficial or low-paying. Those little jobs sometimes lead to bigger and better assignments."
- Solicit businesses and publications that are thriving in this economy. Right now, greeting card sales are up, for example. People are eating more sweets and other comfort foods. American flags are a booming business.
- Write speeches. CEOs and association leaders often hire speechwriters. If you have a knack for speechwriting, read the local calendar of events in the newspaper to find out who is speaking and where. Attend speeches and presentations. Join or

visit organizations and get involved at the district and state level where you'll meet men and women who hire speechwriters.

- Advertise your services. Build a Web site or join an organization such as NAWW (National Association of Women Writers – www.naww.org) or SPAWN (Small Publishers, Artists and Writers Network – www.spawn.org) and get Web site space where you can receive recognition for your work. Send out brochures to local businesses or a targeted mailing list.
- Ensure greater success during difficult times by establishing and maintaining a good reputation all the time.

# Research Techniques for Writers

Like it or not, writing involves research. As a writer of nonfiction articles and books, I spend a lot of my time doing research. Most fiction writers must also do research—to learn about the town where their story takes place or to understand facets of their character's career, for example. Even poets conduct research occasionally—to determine the color pattern of a specific bird or to find an appropriate quote, perhaps.

I guess that's why I'm always surprised when a writer sends me a question that requires research as if they don't know how to access the information themselves. But then, asking someone who knows is also a form of research.

Sometimes, however, I don't have a definitive answer to a writer's question. So, when someone asks, "How many words should I write for a mystery book?" "What steps can I take to get started as a grant writer?" "What is creative nonfiction?" "How much should I charge for ghost writing a book?" I do what that writer could do—research.

My research techniques vary according to the type of information I need. In the case of the appropriate number of words for a mystery book, my instinct told me that this would vary from publisher to publisher. I wanted to either verify or nullify my own conclusion. I queried a literary agent who handles mysteries and a couple of publishers who publish them. I learned that, while there is a range one should stay within when writing a mystery, the numbers will change from publisher to publisher. Thus, I advised the writer to stay within the suggested range, to study each publisher's Guidelines for Writers and to be willing to adapt her mystery for the particular publisher who wants to view it.

When asked to define creative nonfiction, I turned to a couple of sources: *Writer's Market* and the Internet. *Writer's Market* has a fairly complete glossary as well as abundant information for writers. And the Internet houses an endless supply of data.

There are five main sources of research today: books, articles, the Internet, professional experts and the ordinary individual with the right sort of experience and/or knowledge.

You can find information and potential experts in books and articles. And you can find out about those books and articles on the Internet. With some Web savvy, you can locate Web sites overflowing with facts, statistics and expert sources as well as individuals to interview on a variety of topics.

Many writers complain, however, "But I can never find what I'm looking for on the Internet." Often these people are lacking the three assets they need: research skills, curiosity and lots of patience. While you're developing these qualities, you can benefit from the following research guide.

In order to search the Web, you must first access a search engine. In the space provided on your screen, type the address for the search engine you wish to use. The most popular search engines include AltaVista, Yahoo and Google. To access any of them, you would type www.altavista.com, www.Yahoo.com or www.google.com.

Once the search engine screen is displayed, type your subject in the space provided and wait for a response. While the Web site with the information you seek sometimes appears right away, other times you'll have to try several different word combinations before you score.

Look through the list of Web sites that appear and click on the one you want to visit. You'll be quickly swept away either to the site that houses the material you wanted or someplace totally unrelated. Be prepared to visit a lot of wrong sites before the right one comes along.

Be specific when choosing your search words. Use descriptive words. If you don't succeed with your choice of words, try another. Use different spellings. Let's say you want information about caring for baby rabbits.

Using *rabbit* as a search word, might bring up a variety of sites unrelated to your interest. This list will include children's books about rabbits, how to show rabbits, various breeds of rabbits, how to get rid of rabbits in your garden and so forth. Instead, you might want to type in, *birthing rabbits* or *baby rabbits* or *bunnies* or *caring for baby rabbits*.

More clearly define your search by using quotation marks. Let's say that you want historical information about the Florida Keys. As an experiment, using AltaVista.com, I typed in *Florida Keys* and received 228,213 listings. Of course, the majority of them had nothing to do with my interest. So I used quotation marks: "Florida Keys" and received 117,796 listings. That was more manageable, but I wanted to refine my search more. I typed "Florida Keys History" and got just 151 more focused site listings. This technique is a real time saver, believe me.

For a more successful search, use the singular version of a word, type in "cat" instead of "cats," for example. Here again, make it clear whether you want to find articles about cat behavior ("cat behavior," "cat personalities," "cat traits"), the number of feral cats in America ("feral cat statistics," "feral cat colonies in America," "wild domestic cats") or a list of cat names ("cat names," "naming a cat").

Experience and practice will help you to fine tune your searches.

Remember, though, there are no regulations for Web sites. Anyone can start a site for any purpose and provide whatever information they want. It's your responsibility as a researcher to double check the information you receive.

Once you get to the site, utilize it in its entirety. Look at the articles, find out about their recommended books, study their various informational pages and click on any appropriate links. I probably find more of the information I need when conducting research, through Web site links than any other single tool or resource.

There are numerous ways to find experts on the Internet. Here are a few:

- Use a search engine to locate an expert by topic, horticulture (horticulturist), animal psychology or psychologist or wildlife photography (photographer), for example.
- Find experts listed in online articles related to your topic.
- Search university staff Web pages to find experts for a variety of topics.
- Locate the names of author experts at www.amazon.com.
- Search for author contact information by author name, by publishing company name or by book title.
- Locate nonprofessional experts through message boards. Type in "your topic + message board." For example, "parent message board" or "pet message board."

Here are a few sites for researchers:

www.yearbooknews.com. Type in your topic and get a list of experts and contact information.

www.inernetstats.com. Provides statistics and the results of surveys related mostly to business.

www.pollingreport.com for trends in public opinion from politics to health to sports and family values

www.grammarnow.com for grammatical help

www.dailyglobe.com/day2day.html. The Daily Globe offers an extensive list of events to help spur those ideas and to help in fleshing out the details in a novel.

www.about.com has a large database where you can look up numerous topics.

www.infoplease.com is the Information Please site.

While Web research may seem overwhelming at first, with practice and persistence, you'll soon come to rely on this means of research. Hang in there and you, too, will become a skilled Web surfer.

# Develop a Successful Writer's Web Site

o writers need Web sites? They do if they have something to sell or a
essage to share. And I guess that includes just about every writer.

our own Web site means exposure to a segment of the population
at you may not already be reaching. It's a place where potential
ients, publishers and editors can learn about you and your work.
nd you can sell your self-published books through a Web site.

ut what should a Web site include? How do you design one that's
ffective? Following are some tips for creating a Web site that successfully
ortrays the message and purpose that you want to express.

: **Research other writers' Web sites**. View these sites to determine
hat features might appeal to the visitors you hope to attract

: **Strive for clarity**. Make sure that those visiting your site know at
 glance what it's about. If you're selling books, state this on your
ome page. If you're advertising your editorial business, post your
ervices front and center. Perhaps you want to create a Web site
here editors and publishers can view samples of your work. Make
is clear on your home page.

: **Keep it Simple**. While conducting Web site research, you'll find
ome interesting site designs with some unusual color combinations.
Before succumbing to the unconventional, consider how it will impact
our audience. Will your visitors be able to read yellow words dancing
cross the page over a turquoise background sprinkled with black
olka dots? Will they wait for the little pencil figure to recite your
atest poem before navigating your site? Don't try to be so clever
hat you defeat your purpose.

lake it easy for folks to move around on your site. I suggest repeating
our list of contents on every page, for example.

4: **Build a strong first impression**. Your home page should be inviting while luring visitors to other areas of your site. If your home page is blah and has no explanation or promise of interesting things to come, busy Web surfers won't bother to look any further.

5: **Exceed visitors' expectations**. While you don't want to clutter up your Web site with unnecessary material, you certainly want to respond to your visitors' needs. If you're selling books, for example, show pictures of them, include a synopsis of each and provide an author bio as well as ordering information. If you're promoting your editorial services, a bio/ resume, references and your photograph would be appropriate. A site designed to showcase your work to editors and publishers should also answer all of their potential questions. You might post your current bio, previously published work, work in progress, letters of recommendation and your photograph.

6: **Advertise your site**. Having a site is only the beginning. In order for it to be effective, you must invite people to visit. Your Web site designer can help you get linked to the most important search engines. You'll also want to exchange links with Web sites expressing themes complimentary to yours. Spend a couple of hours each week seeking out good link prospects.

Tell people about your site. Include your Web site address (URL) on your letterhead and business cards. Add a *signature* to your outgoing emails. A signature is a message that you can have automatically placed at the bottom of each email you send.

Who should you get to design your Web site and how much will you have to pay? When I asked Web site designer and SPAWN Webmaster, Virginia Lawrence, Ph. D this question, she said, "You can get the kid next door to do it for a couple of pizzas or you can spend a million dollars or any amount in between." The minimum you can expect to pay an experienced professional to design a basic Web site is probably around $500.

Of course, you can build your own site and there are programs to help Lawrence recommends HotMetal. She says, "A lot of people like reamweaver." But she suggests that beginners stay away from ontPage. She says, "It creates pages with all kinds of unnecessary tra junk."

nother option is to do what I did and arrange for a Web design student build your site as a class project. It was a win-win situation. I have a ry nice Web site and the student earned a good grade while learning a ade.

o you need a Web site? If you're a working writer, the answer is obably, "yes."

## *Chapter Ten*

..........................

*How to Build Your Writing Business*

♦**Keep Those New Year's Resolutions**

♦**Stop Procrastinating Now!**

♦**Spring Cleaning for Writers**

# Keep Those New Year's Resolutions

(While this article is helpful anytime that you want to start anew, it is especially useful to read right around the New Year.)

It's time, once again, to take stock of your accomplishments. Did you meet all of your goals for the year? Did you finish that book, send twenty query letters to magazines each month or start working on your memoirs? If so, CONGRATULATIONS! Keep up the good work. If not, you aren't alone. Millions of people break their New Year's resolutions and this is generally because they set their standards too high.

Perhaps you can achieve success by lowering your sights. You have a very good chance of failure if you resolve to write a best seller, double your income and earn the Pulitzer Prize by year's end, for example. If you've never put pen to paper, perhaps a more realistic goal would be to spend three hours each day writing, enroll in a writing class and subscribe to a couple of writing publications. And then be willing to step outside your comfort zone.

It's like the woman who asked me to help her get over a serious writing slump. She hadn't been able to write a meaningful word in months. She said that she wanted to get back to her poetry and short story writing yet, she wasn't willing to make the necessary lifestyle changes. I suggested that she write for at least ten minutes each day in her journal. She saw no point in doing that when she really wanted to write poetry. I said, "Then write poetry for ten minutes each day." She replied, "I can't do that. I told you I'm in a slump."

I advised her to spend those ten minutes just sitting quietly or walking in a lovely setting. I said that if she did this each day, she would soon become inspired and she would start using this time to write. She said that was impossible—she had no time during the day to be quiet and by evening, her mind raced so fast, she could not get into a relaxed state. Obviously, until this woman is ready to make some changes, she will continue to fail.

re you going to spend the rest of your life watching others enjoy the festyle you desire or are you going to make this the year you claim success or yourself? Here are some typical writers' resolutions and some plans to elp you get started on an adventure toward meeting your personal and rofessional goals.

**. Finish that book (poem, article, story)**. Pick up your work-in-rogress now, while the year is new and you still have that great sense of tarting fresh. But don't look at this as one humungous project because ou'll feel overwhelmed. Take baby steps. Tackle this one page, one stanza, ne paragraph at a time. Break it down into phases. For a book, you night vow to write a chapter each month. For a story, start with the outline, evelop the characters, research the time period and then start the writing. These tasks might be scheduled over a period of a week or, if working on t only part-time, a month or two.

**. Start a writing project that you've been wanting to pursue.** imilar to the steps in the first resolution, figure out how much time it will ake, how much time you want to devote per day/week and just start. )ne thing is for sure, if you don't start it, you will never finish it. Make his the year you stop procrastinating. If you have several projects and lon't know which one to work on, use the list method. List the pros and he cons of starting each project at this time. The right one will become evident in your list.

**. Approach at least one new market for your writing each month**. Expand your horizons. If you typically write how-to pieces for parenting, general and health magazines, try your hand at a profile piece for a business publication, for example. Maybe you design brochures for local businesses. Increase your business and your expertise by offering to write their company newsletters. I know a writer who was earning a steady income writing PR material for a large healthcare firm. Last year, she decided to try something different and she has since sold three personal essays to a major woman's magazine for a total sum of $4,000.

**4. Try one new book promotion idea per month.** If you're an autho you already know that there's more to selling a book than having it i Barnes and Noble. Read my book, *Over 75 Good Ideas for Promotin Your Book* and John Kremer's book featuring 1001 book promotio ideas and apply some of these ideas to your promotional repertoire thi year. Arrange to sell your book through local independent bookstore and gift shops. Send press releases with order forms to libraries throughou the U.S. Record your book on tape for the blind and the busy. Do som piggyback marketing. I once procured a booth at the county fair to promo my local history book. Of course, I sold scads more than I would had stayed home that week.

**5. Write something different.** As professional writers, we sometime neglect our creative urges. We are so busy writing articles, working o clients' books or writing company materials that we don't get around t satisfying our own writing cravings. This year, reward yourself more. Se aside an hour a day or an entire afternoon each week to write poetry, t work on your novel or even to do more journaling.

**6. Join a community or online writers' group.** My career accelerate when I finally left my writing cubical and began connecting with othe writers. I found the camaraderie and the support extremely nurturing and still do. I can't even calculate the educational value. If you want t reap the benefits of networking with other writers, start looking for local or online organization. Be a loyal participant. Bring what you ca to the meetings or to the discussions and share it in exchange for all tha you will glean.

**7. Add a new dimension to your lifestyle.** If you are a full-time writer you're probably at the computer day in and day out. You enjoy you work immensely, but sometimes feel on the verge of burnout. This year establish some pleasurable time away from your office. Do more reading Get involved in something creative such as, mosaic or scrapbooking. Start playing tennis. And then pursue this activity at least a couple o times a week.

**8. Volunteer more.** It feels good to reach out and help someone. And there are a lot of projects writers can do within the community. Here are a few: Volunteer for the after school homework help program at your local library. Offer to mentor a journalism student or adult who is just starting a writing career. Start a writing club. Volunteer to write the fund raising material for a charity dear to your heart.

**9. Make a gift of your writing.** There are numerous ways to give through your writing. Make your own Christmas and greeting cards. Personalized cards are always appreciated. Write one of your poems in calligraphy, frame it and give it to a friend or family member. Create a book of your short stories and have it bound at Kinkos or a print-on-demand company. Write a children's story starring the children in your life and give it to them for their birthdays. Maybe you know someone who can add charming drawings or photographs. For Christmas, I gather all of my published articles for that year, put them in binders and wrap them up for my three daughters and my parents. I know they enjoy this unique gift because one year I didn't get around to putting the articles together for them and boy did I hear about it. They enjoy seeing the versatility and scope of my work and to have this ongoing keepsake.

Use some of these unique ways to help you keep your New Year's resolutions. The result will be a happier more productive you throughout the coming year.

# Stop Procrastinating Now!

What is the most common obstacle to your success? Many would-be writers consider procrastination to be their biggest roadblock and their greatest productivity thief.

But why do we put off tasks that we know we should be doing and often genuinely want to do?

Sometimes it's a matter of sloppy organizational skills. We simply can't get to it because of poor planning or faulty scheduling. A more common reason is fear—fear of the process of the task, ("Am I really capable of doing this?") or the outcome ("What if I fail?" or What if I succeed?"). We might procrastinate when we feel overwhelmed by the scope of a project. And sometimes procrastination stems from a sense of rebellion ("I won't let that task dictate how I'll spend my time and energy"). Perfectionists tend to procrastinate when they fear that their efforts might be considered merely mediocre ("If I can't do it to perfection, I won't do it at all").

We all procrastinate sometimes. If you occasionally drag your feet before starting a writing assignment, you probably don't have a problem. However, if you continually miss deadlines and often agonize over the work that you should be doing, you may be at risk of procrastinating your writing career into oblivion.

## Explore Your Procrastination Triggers

Do you currently have a writing job on your desktop that you've been putting off? Visualize yourself tackling that project. How does it feel? Do you experience any sort of discomfort when you think about that task—fear, nervousness, guilt or anger, for example? Examine why you are guilty, angry, nervous or afraid.

Once you know why you procrastinate—when you understand what created the hurdles and roadblocks—you can take steps toward overcoming them. Perhaps you're resisting starting the next chapter in your memoirs. And when you think about it, your eyes well up with tears. You may be procrastinating to avoid the emotional onslaught of the material slotted for that chapter. Once you know that your emotions are stopping you, you can take steps to prepare yourself for the task.

## Turn Those Pesky "Shoulds" into Choices

Sometimes we avoid a task as an act of rebellion. The more it seems to press for our attention, the more we resist. No one likes to be a victim of the "shoulds" in life. If you're feeling pressure to start a particular writing assignment, don't surrender. Take charge. Realize that you have choices. You've made one choice not to start the assignment. You can make a new choice at any time. Take back your power and exercise your choices.

## Start at the Beginning, or Not

We tend to procrastinate when we feel overwhelmed by the scope of a writing project. One might whine, "I just don't know where to start." I usually suggest starting at the beginning. I've learned many times over that one baby step and then another and another can lead to the completion of even an enormous project.

Sometimes it's necessary to go in the backdoor and that's okay, too. If it's more comfortable for you to start somewhere in the middle, go for it. Perhaps you want to outline your article before conducting research and interviews. Maybe you need to write your last chapter first. It really doesn't matter where you start as long as you move off dead center.

## Learn How to Prioritize

For many writers, a procrastination problem is really a prioritization problem. Maybe this will help: List the projects you have on the table, now—everything that must be accomplished by the end of the day, week or month. Give the most important tasks a one rating, the next in line of importance, a two and so forth.

Now transfer all of the number one rated tasks to the top of a new list. Follow with the number two tasks and so forth. Note how much time each one will take and create a schedule designed to accomplish them.

You may have to adjust your schedule occasionally as new projects with higher priority come into your life. Also, for greater efficiency, let projects overlap. You might be conducting research for an article with a July 1st deadline and sending out a few query letters while writing an article due on May 15 and revising one scheduled for the end of May.

## Create a Clear Pathway

Those who procrastinate are not happy. They have guilt pulling at them day after day for as long as they put off the dreaded task. But sometimes the problem is as simple as all of those smaller jobs cluttering your desk. You aren't overwhelmed by the pending project, but by the everyday tasks that seem to be piling up all around you. The solution; take a day to clear the clutter in your life and you'll create a pathway to the project at hand.

# Spring Cleaning For Writers

Most of us know that fresh feeling that comes after doing our spring-cleaning. It's like experiencing the rebirth of our home. Wouldn't it be great if you could experience the same sense of renewal in your writing career? You can. Here are some ideas to help you clear the cobwebs from your mental and physical space and refurbish your creativity.

**Clear the clutter.** Do you have folders stacked on top of the filing cabinet waiting to be filed? Is your desktop buried under paperwork? Are your in/out baskets overflowing? Do you have to step over books and other research material to go get a cup of coffee? Are you having trouble putting your hands on the documents you need? Do you fear that your cat will get lost in the rubble of your office? If so, it's time to get out the shovel—er... a... the broom. Here's a tip: Concentrate on expanding the organizational systems that are working in your office and eliminating those that are not.

**Review your goals and set new ones.** Now that your writing space is organized, it's time to clear the clutter from your head. Perhaps you've been working on several projects at once and you're feeling overwhelmed. Maybe you've worked on the same project for months and feel burned out. Having a clean, clutter-free space will help to lift your spirits, but it's also necessary to tackle the clutter in your mind. List current and future projects. Set reasonable deadlines and design a plan for meeting them. When you're aware of the steps necessary to complete a project, you can more easily move toward that goal.

**Educate yourself.** Learn something new about writing or marketing works in your genre. Subscribe to a writing-oriented magazine or ezine. Join a writing/publishing-related organization or trade club. Take steps to hone your speaking or marketing skills. Stagnation is murder on creativity.

**Try something new.** Maybe this is the time to try out a new genre or to shift from writing articles or short stories to writing a book. Find out about some of the current trends, come up with a good story idea and pitch it to a new editor. If you've been writing on parenting issues, try your hand at a piece aimed at teachers, mentors, religious leaders or children, for example. Remember that a writer who doesn't stretch, doesn't grow.

**Expand your writing into other fields**. While you've been busily writing about building birdhouses, needlework or home computing, you've been gaining expertise. Make this experience work for you by becoming a teacher, consultant or Web presence, for example.

**Find new ways to market your work**. Most writers would rather not spend their precious time in marketing mode. Marketing is necessary for those of us who want to sell our work, however. This spring, step outside your comfort zone and explore new ways to market yourself and your work. Start by updating your resume, business brochure and other promotional material. Approach new editors with your article and story ideas. Recycle your articles and stories through reprints. Come up with new ideas for promoting your book (contact radio talk show hosts or the directors for related organizations, for example).

Follow these tips and your writing career will blossom like a fresh spring bloom in the morning sunshine.

# Chapter Eleven

..................................

## Taking Care of the Writer Within

♦ **Journal-keeping For Writers**

♦ **A Writer's Garden**

♦ **The Care and Feeding of the Whole Writer**

# Journal-Keeping for Writers

There's no better way for a writer to start the flow of creative juices than by writing. That's just one reason why so many writers keep a journal.

Journaling is often more relaxing and meaningful than the writing you do for a living. You're not writing under pressure. You can take writing risks because no one else is going to read it. In the process, you will hone your writing skills and discover your literary strengths. Through journal-keeping, writers can reinvent themselves as writers.

Following are some creative and useful ways you can use your journal:

**Work through writer's block**. We all suffer the curse of the dreaded blank screen syndrome from time to time. The next time it happens to you, turn to your journal. For this exercise, I suggest using a journal book instead of your computer. Get away from your desk and start writing by hand.

Let the words flow without thinking about them. Don't worry about sentence structure and grammar; just write whatever comes to mind. If you need a jumpstart, choose a topic. Describe the room you're in, an object within your view or your cat, for example. Write about a recent outing that you enjoyed—a day at the shore, a hike or a shopping spree. Once the words are flowing nicely, turn your attention to the topic that had you blocked earlier. Focus your thoughts and your writing on that subject and you may be surprised at what pearls will appear.

**Clear the clutter from your mind**. A writer must learn to set everything else aside in order to focus on the work at hand. If there's something keeping you from concentrating on your work, write about it.

Try this technique: Write about whatever is on your mind. Just let the words roll out. If you can type faster than you can write, you may want to do this exercise on the computer. Some of your words will make sense and others may not. Don't stop to analyze your words. Just keep writing/typing. If you already know what is hanging you up, this is a good way to

t it off your chest. If you don't know what is bothering you, keep writing
d it will eventually be revealed. Then you can most likely return to work
eling less burdened and more productive.

**oothe the pain of rejection.** A writer with any ambition at all, will face
jection. It's a fact of the working writer's life. It's also a fact that
metimes rejection will get you down. When this happens, turn to your
urnal. Start by documenting your successes—the article you sold last
eek, your published book, your third place award in the recent short
ory contest, the complimentary review about your book online and the
her three articles that have been requested this month. Raise your spirits
y writing about your achievements instead of dwelling on rejection.

**esolve problems.** Journaling is an excellent decision-making tool.
Vriting about a problem is more effective than simply thinking about it,
ecause thoughts tend to just keep circling around in your head. Write
own your thoughts, feelings and ideas about a situation. You'll gain a new
erspective and the way will be cleared to a solution.

et's say that you are undecided about whether to take a part-time job.
ist the pros and cons. After examining your list, highlight those items that
re most significant to you. While making more money is important, you
night decide that being home with your children, doing what you love and
aving the opportunity to express your creativity holds more meaning for
ou at this time.

**ncrease creativity**. A journal can be your creative outlet. Let's say that
ou spend your days designing brochures for business clients or writing
onfiction articles and you yearn to write poetry or short stories. Use your
urnal to express yourself through poetry. Devote a section of your journal
story ideas. Draw or sketch images representing your thoughts
hroughout the pages of your journal.

**oost your confidence.** A journal can help to keep your spirits up. Here's
ny favorite technique: Establish a *Me* page in your journal. Write about
he happy things in your life (your family, a beloved pet, wonderful friends,
lovely home and good health). List your accomplishments (the ability to

ski, the fact that you're a published author, winning first place on your jam at the county fair, an honorable mention in the short story contest two years ago). Visit this page whenever your confidence is sagging.

**Chart your course.** A journal can be your life story, a book of memories or a collection of your dreams. It's a safe place to express your most private thoughts and to work through your most difficult dilemmas. A journal is a roadmap outlining where you've been which, in turn, will help you to determine where you're going. And this can be a valuable tool in the success of you're writing career

# A Writer's Garden

I didn't know how important creative outlets were for a working writer until I took up gardening with a more artistic eye.

I had always taken care of a yard—I mowed lawns and tended flowers. But a few years ago I took this interest a step further and planted a vegetable garden. The pleasure and satisfaction that came from preparing the soil, planting seeds, nurturing the plants, harvesting the vegetables and bringing them to the table was incredible. I'll never forget the Thanksgiving that I served pies made from pumpkins that grew in my little garden.

My garden is my sanctuary when I need a break from the office. It's where I vent—have you ever pulled weeds to release frustrations? It gives my hands and heart new purpose and brings me pleasure.

If you'd like a garden where you can express your creativity, spend pockets of time away from your work, enjoy serenity or even work out some of your problems, here's what I recommend:

**Start small**. Choose just one area to transform—maybe a plot within view of your office or a long neglected garden bed. For instant gratification, plant seedlings or plants. For summer splash, plant a package of sunflower or wildflower seeds. You can grow a few carrots, onions, beans, beets or tomatoes in a fairly small, sunny space. I even plant a winter vegetable garden. During the months of March and April, I enjoy snow peas (pea pods) in salads, sautéed as a side dish and as a healthy snack. I grow about a dozen snow pea plants in a narrow space measuring four feet long.

**Garden smart**. There are numerous ways to approach your garden project. You can make it as simple or as complex as you want. Go to the nursery and select an array of flowers or veggies that you love and just plant them. Or draw up a plan for planting based on careful study and research. If you're new to gardening, I suggest you invest in a good garden book so you'll know which seeds to plant during which season, how much space they'll need and whether they prefer sun or shade, for example.

If money is an issue, plant a friendship garden. Swap plants with friends and neighbors or transplant things that are already growing in your own yard.

**Lead with your heart.** Have fun with your garden. I intermingle veggies and flowers, for example. My gardens might include lavender, nasturtiums, calendula, sweet peas and a potted miniature rose with rows of cabbage, onions, string beans and a few squash and tomato plants. There's usually a sunflower or two coming up in the spring, as well.

**Bring together the things you love.** I like using birdhouses, birdfeeders and other yard ornaments in my gardens. Some gardeners incorporate artwork among their plants—sculptures, mosaic items and so forth.

I recently planted a small space outside my office window in pale shades of lavender and pink pansies, stalk and alyssum. I used a cat-shaped stepping stone in the little flower bed and placed a garden fairy statue there. Because I can't see the garden when I'm sitting at my desk, I hung a pot of pansies at window level on a shepherd's hook. I also placed a hummingbird feeder above the pansy pot. My cats and I all enjoy the frequent visits from hummingbirds throughout the day.

**Design a meditation or contemplation garden.** Set aside a garden space large enough that you can create the illusion of privacy. Place a small bench there among plants and shrubs that calm and delight you. I suggest planting things in varying heights, textures and colors. Plant something fragrant and plants that rustle in the breeze. Add a water feature, decorative rocks and, perhaps a bird feeder or two. If you choose low maintenance plants, you can spend more time in meditation and less in tending the garden.

**Attract wildlife.** If you enjoy birds, butterflies and other wildlife, plant things that will attract them. Butterflies like lavender, for example. Birds are drawn to plants with berries. Research the birds and butterflies in your area and choose plants that will bring them in.

**Plant a memory garden**. Incorporate things you remember your parents or your grandparents growing. I'm particular fond of pansies because my grandmother enjoyed them.

**Grow an herb garden**. There are so many lovely and fragrant herbs that grow quite easily even in a small space. Carry your creativity to a new level by using herbs in cooking, teas, craft projects and for medicinal purposes

**Do container gardening.** You can create the illusion of a garden inside or on a small patio or balcony with potted plants. Grow a backdrop of bamboo or another attractive plant in large pots. Plant smaller containers full of colorful flowering plants or an array of interesting succulents. In a sunny spot, you can even grow a small salad garden in containers.

What is a writer's garden? It's where a writer can express his/her creativity through the process of gardening or where he/she can go to relax. If you enjoy gardening or simply spending time in a garden, consider establishing your writer's garden.

# The Care and Feeding
## of the Whole Writer

Do you sometimes feel that you're one-dimensional? Are you so singularly focused on writing that you have little interest or energy left for any of life's other offerings? Is your passion for writing making you sick? Yes sick—the stress and strain of sitting for hours, sleeplessness, improper diet and lack of variety can take its toll on your health.

You know this. But it's hard to get away from that novel, those articles or that client work. If you're trying to earn a living through writing, you don't have time for anything else and you don't want to do anything else.

A body, even one with a heart for writing, needs balance. When you eat right, rest enough, exercise regularly, pursue a hobby, avail yourself of mental stimulation, engage in social activities, find your spiritual center and volunteer, you become more complete. And you will be a more effective writer.

Following are some ideas and techniques for creating more balance in your life.

**Get eight hours of zzzzz's**. Burning the midnight oil is a good way to suffer mental and physical burn out. Establish a regular routine that involves six to eight hours of uninterrupted sleep every night. If you're a morning person, get up at 5, but make sure you're in bed by 9 or 10 that evening. If you prefer writing late at night, sleep in until 7 or 8 in the morning and stop working by 11 or 12 that night.

**Eat your veggies**. You know the drill—consume more fruits, vegetables, whole grains and legumes than chips, cookies and donuts. If you tend to eat on the run, spend a few minutes each morning laying out your day's meals like you would your child's school clothes. Make a tuna and spinach sandwich on whole wheat and pack it with an apple for lunch. Cut fresh, crisp veggies to serve with homemade garbanzo bean dip for snacks. Make a large salad every three days and eat it for lunch. Keep cartons of yogurt on hand. Bananas are great snacking food. I slice one on my oatmeal each morning and eat that at my desk for breakfast. Drink a lot of water throughout the day. This will help keep your energy level up. Eat (and drink) smart and you will be surprised how much more productive you'll be.

**Get moving**. You've heard it before—physical activity increases circulation which improves your thought process and gives you more energy. It doesn't matter whether you call it working out, fitness training or conditioning, just do it. Find a mode of exercise that you can embrace—preferably outside in the fresh air. Walk, run, bicycle, swim, jump rope, lift weights, shoot hoops, play racquetball, use a rowing machine or take up tap dancing and do it on a regular basis. Walking is my exercise of choice. I walk everyday for a change of mental and physical pace. I use this 45-minute walking break to collect my thoughts and work through any problems. It's an uplifting experience and I generally return to my desk feeling recharged and refreshed.

**Take regular breaks**. Long-time dedicated writers typically suffer from repetitive stress discomfort, stiffness in the shoulders-neck area or leg problems. My chiropractor is always reminding me to avoid sitting for long periods. Put variety in your daily schedule so you're not working in the same position for hours at a time. Type for a while and then water the houseplants, for example. Do some research, take a walk and then make a few phone calls. Type again before breaking for lunch. Your afternoon might consist of more writing, responding to email, additional research, out-of-office errands, some filing and bookwork. While we're on the subject, make sure your workstation is ergonomically sound—that your computer screen is at the right height, keyboard at the correct angle, chair facing the keyboard and computer screen and that you sit up straight while working.

**Seek mental stimulation and inspiration**. Read for pleasure and learning. Spend time with interesting people. Attend lectures and social events. See good movies and plays. Join a club or organization. Pursue a few activities outside of your writing world and just watch your business increase. You'll return with fresh ideas and maybe even a new approach to work.

**Expand your creative endeavors**. The most joy-filled writers I know have other creative outlets. One makes jewelry, another works with clay, others pursue gardening, needlework or carpentry. It was fairly recent that I discovered the value of a creative hobby for writers. Working or playing at something new stretches the mind and boosts those creative juices. Success in any pursuit is satisfying. After thirty minutes spent tending my vegetable garden, pansy bed or orchids, I return to work with a new outlook. After a day of intense writing work, I love to relax with a needlepoint project before going to bed.

**Acknowledge your spirituality**. Attend church, read inspirational books, join a prayer group or spend time in meditation. A spiritual connection helps to soothe emotional wounds, it keeps you feeling more well grounded and brings you a greater sense of peace.

**Help others**. I know, I know, you don't have time to volunteer. You have deadlines to meet and there are sonnets dancing around in your head that need to come out. Sometimes volunteering isn't any more time consuming than stepping outside and helping an elderly neighbor bring in her groceries. I operate a full-time writing business and also volunteer with five organizations. I sit on the local historic preservation commission. I gather donated items for a rescue cat organization and help out there with the kittens on occasion. I judge a youth speaking contest each year for the Optimist club, I do some writing and respond to questions for two writing organizations. And, last year, I became a mentor to a 13-year-old girl. People ask, "Doesn't this take away from your writing?" After thinking about it, I have to say, "No, it greatly enhances my writing."

How do you define yourself? Do you say, "I'm a writer?" Expand your concept of yourself. Add balance to your lifestyle—become more well rounded. Not only will you be a better writer, you'll become a more interesting person.

# Chapter Twelve

........................

*Resources for Writers and Independent Publishers*

♦Books for Writers and Publishers
♦Magazines, Ezines and Newsletters
♦General Sites for Writers and
IndependentPublishers
♦Sites for Children's Writers
♦Christian Writing Sites
♦Sites for Poets
♦Sites for Travel Writers
♦Sites for Fiction Writers
♦Science Fiction Writer's Sites
♦Markets and Jobs for Writers
♦Experts, Surveys and Statistics
♦General Research Sites
♦Newspaper Listings
♦Grammar Sites
♦Resources for Independent Publishers
♦Information and Forms for Publishers
♦Ebook Publishing and POD
♦Book Review Sites
♦Online Bookstores
♦Business and Tax Help for Writers
♦Help Finding an Agent
♦Grants for Writers
♦Warnings

# Resources For Writers and Independent Publishers

As writers and publishers, we are constantly in need of new information and resources. It takes more than being a talented writer to succeed. It also takes good research skills.

Not only do I conduct research for the many articles and books I write, I also compile the monthly *Market Update* for the SPAWN Web site. Through this online publication, I report industry trends, feature writer/editor/publisher interviews and list numerous resources for writers, artists and publishers. I'm happy to share the following resources with you. I hope you use them to enhance your own research skills. (Refer to page 145 for a step-by-step guide to becoming a skilled researcher.)

## Books for Writers and Publishers

*A Writer's Guide to Magazine Articles for Book Promotion and Profit*, Patricia Fry (Matilija Press). This 66-page book offers an easy-to-follow guide to getting your articles published. (www.matilijapress.com)

*Over 75 Good Ideas for Promoting Your Book*, Patricia Fry (Matilija Press). Here are oodles of no and low cost ideas for promoting your book. (www.matilijapress.com)

*The Author's Tool Kit*, Mary Embree (Allworth Press). A step-by-step guide to writing and publishing your book.

*The Self Publishing Manual*, Dan Poynter (Para Publishing). The self-publisher's Bible.

*Writer's Market* (Writer's Digest Books). Contains listings for over 8,000 book publishers and magazine editors.

## Magazines, Ezines and Newsletters

*Writer's Digest*—print magazine found on newsstands and at www.writersdigest.com

*The Writer*—print magazine found on newsstands and at www.writermag.com

*Freelance Writer's Report*—print newsletter. To order, call 603-922-8338 or go to www.writers-editors.com

*Writers' Journal*—print magazine. To order, call 218-346-7921 or go to www.writersjournal.com

*SPAWNews*—free online newsletter produced by Small Publishers, Artists and Writers Network (www.spawn.org)
*NAWW Weekly*—online newsletter for the National Association of Women Writers (www.naww.org)
*Writing World* (www.writing-world.com)
*Writers Weekly* (www.writersweekly.com)
*WriterOnline* (www.writeronline.com)

## General Sites for Writers and Independent Publishers
SPAWN—Small Publishers, Artists and Writers Network (www.spawn.org)
National Association of Women Writers—NAWW (www.naww.org)
Writing-World (www.writing-world.com)
Writing for Dollars (www.writingfordollars.com)
Write Thinking (www.writethinking.net
Writer's Guild of America (www.wga.org)
My Writer Buddy (www.mywriterbuddy.com)
Wooden Horse Publishing (www.woodenhorsepub.com)

## Sites for Children's Writers
Children's Writers Marketplace (www.write4kids.com)
Society of Children's Book Writers and Illustrators (www.scbwi.org)
Writing for Children (www.writingforchildren.co.uk)

## Christian Writing Sites
Christian Writer's Guild (www.christianwritersguild.com)
Resources for Christian Writers (www.bluejaypub.com)
Christian Writers Fellowship (www.cwfi-online.org)

## Sites for Poets
Poetic Voices (www.poeticvoices.com)
Every Poet (www.everypoet.com)
Poetry.com (www.poetry.com)
Poets and Writers (www.pw.org)

## Sites for Travel Writers
TravelWriters (www.travelwriters.com)
Society of American Travel Writers (www.satw.org)

## Sites for Fiction Writers
Fiction addiction (www.fictionaddiction.com)
Fiction Fix (www.coffeehouseforwriters.com)
Fiction Factor (www.fictionfactor.com)
Fiction Connection (www.fictionwriters.com)
Pure Fiction (www.purefiction.com)
Zeotrope: All Story (www.all-story.com)

## Science Fiction Writers' Sites
Science Fiction Writers of America (www.sfwa.org)
Science Fiction Resources (www.members.iinet.net.au/~hooker)

## Markets and Jobs For Writers
Wooden Horse Publishing (www.woodenhorsepub.com)
Writer's Market Online (www.writersmarket.com)
Writerfind (www.writerfind.com)
The Write Jobs (www.writerswrite.com/jobs)
www.sunoasis.com

## Experts, Surveys and Statistics
www.internetstats.com
www.demographics.com
www.pollingreport.com
www.yearbooknews.com
www.expertcentral.com
www.expertclick.com
www.askanexpert.com

## General Research Sites
www.dailyglobe.com/day2day.html
www.yearbooknews.com
www.about.com
www.infoplease.com

## Newspaper Listings
NewspaperLinks.com (www.newspaperlinks.com)
Newspapers.com (www.newspapers.com)
Online Newspapers Worldwide (www.onlinenewspapers.com)

## Grammar Sites
Bartleby.com (www.bartleby.com)
Daily Grammar (www.dailygrammar.com)
SharpWriter.com (www.sharpwriter.com)
Vocabula Review (www.vocabula.com)
Grammar Now (www.grammarnow.com)

## Resources for Independent Publishers
Para Publishing (www.parapub.com)
Small Publishers, Artists and Writers Network (www.spawn.org)
Publishers Marketing Association (www.pma-online.org)

## Information and Forms for Publishers
U.S. Copyright Office
Library of Congress
101 Independence Avenue S.E.
Washington, DC 20559-6000
(www.loc.gov/copyright)

R.R. Bowker
Data Collection Center (for ABI)
POB 6000
Oldsman, Fl 34677-6800
(www.bowker.com )

General Information (ISBN)
630 Central Ave.
New Providence, NJ 07974
 (www.isbn.org)

Quality Books
1003 W. Pines Road
Oregan, Il 61061-9680
(www.quality-books.com)

## Ebook Publishing and POD
Booklocker.com (www.booklocker.com)
1stBooks (www.1stbooks.com)
Virtual Bookworm (www.virtualbookworm.com)

## Book Review Sites
Bookviews (www.bookviews.com)
Book Reporter (www.bookreporter.com)
Book Review Club (www.bookreviewclub.com)

## Online Bookstores
Amazon.com (www.amazon.com)
Barnes and Noble.com (www.barnesandnoble.com)
Fetchbook.com (www.fetchbook.com)
ISBN (Search book titles) www.isbn.nu

## Business and Tax Help for Writers
The Pauper (www.thepauper.com)
Taxes (www.writetools.com/taxes.html)

## Help Finding an Agent
Association of Author's Representatives (www.aar-online.org)
Agent research (www.agentresearch.com)
Writers Net (www.writers.net)

## Grants for Writers
www.fundsforwriters.com

## Warnings
Writer Alerts (www.nwu.org/alerts/alrthome.htm)
Writers Weekly (www.writersweekly.com/warnings/warnings.html)

# Index